The Lucky Ones

A SURVIVOR'S STORY

April 27, 2022
James (Jimi)
Delorme

JIMI DELORME

The Lucky Ones
Copyright © 2021 by Jimi Delorme

All rights reserved. No part of this publication may be reproduced, distributed, or transmitted in any form or by any means, including photocopying, recording, or other electronic or mechanical methods, without the prior written permission of the author, except in the case of brief quotations embodied in critical reviews and certain other non-commercial uses permitted by copyright law.

Tellwell Talent
www.tellwell.ca

ISBN
978-0-2288-6533-9 (Paperback)
978-0-2288-6534-6 (eBook)

Introduction

I am a sixty-five-year-old survivor who spent a total of eleven painful years in the system now recognized as the Canadian government's participation in the genocide against First Nations people. Like hundreds of thousands of other First Nations children, I too was forced to attend these schools against my will.

Despite all the abuse that was not only endured but witnessed by me, I have chosen not to turn this book into a hate-filled rant against the government and churches responsible for the abuses carried out against our people. Instead, I have chosen to focus on the Healing Journey that I chose for myself in order to move forward in a healthy and positive manner.

Yes, the story talks openly about the dark side of what happened in residential schools. I believe this is a necessary part of the healing process. It also helps the public understand the scope of this unthinkable tragedy, just now making its way into the spotlight.

The public has always known about these boarding schools, but in the past most people had no idea about the amount of abuse happening there. When they did speak about the schools, they did so only in whispers. When stories did make it out, they were simply brushed off and treated as nothing more than rumours, just the overactive imaginations of First Nations children who did not like being there.

The public believed that because these schools were being run by their churches, they had to be good places. This is an argument I have heard over and over again from the non-Native people I have lived and worked with.

This book is focused on the difficult Healing Journey that followed my eleven years in those schools. I like to tell people this is a story of survival rather than the abuse most people see when they read it. The most important part of the story is that I am still here, able to tell my story in my own words. I want you all to know that my Healing Journey will last for the rest of my natural life, and it will only reach its conclusion when the Creator sees fit to call me home.

All My Relations!
Ta'wacine O'hitika

Preface

Over the past thirty-two years, I have had the honour and the absolute privilege of working with, as well as learning from, some of the most patient, caring, and humble First Nations Elders that Turtle Island has to offer. Thanks to each of these caring individuals and their spiritual teachings, I am now able to sit here today filled with pride, because I can honestly tell everyone who will listen that I have lived substance-free throughout this entire thirty-two-year period.

From the moment I was introduced to the various spiritual and cultural teachings they all offered so freely, I was fascinated and wanted to know more. Within a matter of days I found myself convinced that this was not only the life I wanted for myself, but it was in fact the life I was truly meant to be living. I quickly learned this was who the Creator meant for me to be, and I should be truly grateful for this gift he has bestowed on me: the life of a First Nations person.

It did not take long before I began to feel that something truly significant and important had been mysteriously awakened within me. I was now able to understand why my life had been in such terrible disarray. It was as though everything around me was in a new and clearer light. I could see all the things I had been oblivious to for years. It was like I was a child again, seeing the outside world for the first time and wanting to see more.

I no longer felt compelled to walk around all day with my head bowed and my eyes locked firmly on the ground because I was ashamed to look people in the eyes, even in passing. I no longer wanted to be quiet about the terrible things that had been done, not only to me, but to thousands of innocent First Nations children before and after me. I felt like a new person with fresh eyes.

Something was telling me I have the ability and the responsibility to speak loudly, to let everyone who will listen know I have not been silenced the way so many others were, the unfortunate ones who did not survive long enough to tell their own stories to the world. They died in one of those awful places, or quietly disappeared with no explanation.

Many of these forgotten children now lie buried in unkept and often unmarked graves at the old school graveyards. Others are still out there, wandering aimlessly through life, lost in that dark and forsaken world of substance abuse and shame, the same awful place I know from many years of personal experience. I consider myself extremely lucky, because I am a survivor.

This is my story.

Kamloops Indian Residential School, where the first 215 unmarked graves opened the eyes of the world to the truth.

Chapter 1

I was approximately five years old when I first began hearing talk about this place, they called *school*. I honestly had no idea of what that entailed; I only knew that I too was eventually going to go there, like it or not. Sometimes the older kids would tease me about it. They would tell me I should have been happy because I was not old enough yet—but my turn was coming soon. This teasing would cause me sudden anxiety about whether or not I really wanted to go to this unknown place.

Aside from the stories I heard from the other kids, I didn't know what to expect from school. I was aware, however, that if I stood on the big armchair in our front room, I could see the other children standing along the main road in front of our small house waiting for that big yellow bus to come and take them away for another day.

When it eventually arrived, my older sister Sharon and all the other local kids would quickly climb on board, laughing, not appearing to be worried about anything. Later that day someone would say, "The kids should be home any time now." This was my cue to head out onto the front steps and patiently wait for the bus to return. Before long it would, and they would all climb off the big yellow bus and run back down the main road, seeming no worse for wear.

This all led me to believe that this *school* must not be as bad as I had thought. In my young mind it appeared to be where everyone went to spend their days playing and having a good time with other kids. After all, everyone seemed happy when they returned at the end of the day. I would sit and watch them as they jumped off the bus and scattered toward their homes, waving at each other and hollering, "See you tomorrow!"

Watching this every day made me so envious that I wanted to go along with my sister right away. However, my mother would always tell me, "You're still too small to go, my boy. maybe next year." I could sense my mother did not want me to go to school. She tried hard to delay the inevitable for as long as she possibly could.

I remember sitting on the floor in the living room of our small home on the reservation, listening to my mother and a small group of local women helping her can berries, mustard beans, and other assorted preserves to help us get through the long winter months. As the women worked, they would often confide in my mother about what was happening in their day-to-day lives. They would take turns giving each other suggestions and ideas about how to deal with whatever problems they were facing.

As I sat there playing with a few small wooden blocks and broken pieces of store-bought toys that someone had liberated from the nearby town dump, I heard one of the ladies talking in an angry tone. She told everyone how she was threatened with jail if she dared refuse to send her little ones to the old mission school down in the valley next year. This was the same school that my older sister and her friends all went to.

The lady told my mother that she felt she had no say whatsoever regarding where she sent her children. She said they had threatened to come in and remove all of her children if she did not comply with what they were asking her to do. They told her it was in the best interest of the children, and the law was on their side, so no one could do anything to stop them from doing their so-called duty. If anyone dared complain about what was happening, they would threaten to call in the local RCMP. This usually quelled all disagreements.

I found out later in life that this was a common tactic used by the people from the Department of Indian Affairs to scare parents into giving up their children without resistance. You also have to remember that a great number of these parents were former residential school students themselves. This meant they too were forcibly removed as children and programmed into submission. They usually did as they were told without question.

Most First Nations people knew that living on the reservation automatically meant that they did not and could not own anything, including their homes or other personal property, such as horses, cattle, or land. Everything was considered property of the Crown or Indian Affairs. Therefore, it only stood to reason that none of them would have any say regarding their children either.

Despite having schools right there on the reserve, most parents knew they had to send their children to the school dictated to them by the Indian Affairs agent in charge of their band or reservation. This single person had absolute power and control over everything that occurred on the reservation. There was not a single corner of the reservation that was out of his reach. Nothing was allowed to happen without his written consent.

In our small reservation community this duty fell to Mr. Simpson, a man everyone tried hard not to offend. He was a short and overweight man in his late fifties, balding with extremely large, hairy ears. He was comical to look at, the way he waddled around in his wrinkled suit at least one or two sizes too small. Still, he was a man people feared.

Most of the people living on the reserve believed that if they stayed in his good books, he would allow their children to go to the reserve day school. However, if you found yourself in his bad books then your children would most likely be sent as far away as possible. He was well aware of the power he had over everyone, and he loved to flaunt it, especially when he had an audience.

According to Mr. Simpson, all the school-aged children were being sent to residential schools because it was in their best interests. He told the parents that we would all get an education, clean clothes, and nutritious meals to eat, along with the education to help us make it in the world. He seemed to believe that we did not get any of these things on the reserve. It was as though he honestly believed that our parents were incapable of bringing up children without guidance from Indian Affairs.

Most of my earliest childhood memories from just prior to residential school surround the days my family worked on a sugar beet farm outside the town of Claresholm, in Southern Alberta. Although I could not have been more than four years old at the time, my memories are clear. My mother would often laugh and say, "I can't believe that you actually remember when you were so young!"

When the adults were off working, we found all sorts of ways to keep ourselves occupied, especially during the hot summer months. Since there were no swimming pools or lakes close by, we would put on our bathing suits or an old pair of cut-offs and walk along one of the many irrigation ditches that ran through the fields. We would each carry an old tire tube or air mattress, and when we were far enough, we would jump on them and ride back to where we started. Most of these irrigation ditches were only about three feet deep, but they ran quite fast depending on whether it had rained the night before.

I recall one incident where I somehow managed to lose my swimming shorts. As we all tried to catch them in the fast-moving current, it became apparent that it was a losing battle. In the end I found myself walking home in the buff, which was met by outbursts of laughter from the adults returning from the fields for supper. Personally, I did not think the situation was funny at all, but the adults all laughed loudly and told me that at least I had managed to hold on to my tire tube.

Our house sat beside the local drive-in movie theatre. We were so close that we could sit in our backyard at night and watch whatever was playing. One of my uncles had gone into the drive-in one night and hooked up speaker wire to one of the speaker posts closest to our house. He ran the wire to our backyard, where he usually parked his car. He must have buried it well, because no one ever mentioned it or made any attempt to disconnect it.

On most nights our mom would let us stay up long enough to watch the cartoons that played before the main feature, then we would all be chased off to bed. Weekends were better because we could stay up later than usual, and someone always made a big bowl of popcorn for us to share. I would fall asleep halfway through the movie, and someone would have to carry me off to bed. This usually fell to one of my aunts.

My memories from that small farming town are mostly pleasant ones. I don't recall experiencing any racist treatment toward me or my siblings. As younger children, the townspeople didn't treat us differently from other neighbourhood kids.

I remember walking along the street picking up bottles as I headed to the small corner store to buy candy. Sometimes people would stop me as I passed their house and hand me a few more bottles, which I gratefully accepted. By the time I reached the corner store I usually had enough to buy myself a pocketful of jawbreakers or bubble gum, which I shared with my siblings.

Our Aunt Louise, my mother's younger sister, worked at the Dairy Queen just up the street from our house. She would often tell us to meet her at the top of the hill at five o'clock. When we got there, she would pass out soft ice cream. Then we would quietly walk our aunt back down the hill to our house, enjoying our ice cream treats.

On the far side of the big field, behind the drive-in, was another big farmhouse, home to a Black family. I can't recall their last name, but they were a large group with more than one generation living under one roof. I often spent my days there playing with their three youngest children, who were around my age. We would play in the loft of their huge barn or on the big tractors and combines parked in the yard.

I do not think they minded having a little brown kid hanging around. When it was mealtime, I was always included at the table set up specifically for the kids. The grandmother would fuss over us and make sure we all had enough to eat. Then we would line up to have our faces and hands wiped with a wet facecloth before being sent back outside to carry on with our activities.

The atmosphere in their home was always warm and caring. I do not remember hearing yelling or scolding. If someone did something they shouldn't have, they would be sat down, usually by the grandmother, and spoken to calmly. When one of us suffered a minor injury while playing, we would be fussed over with great care. The only other time I recall feeling this sense of caring was visiting our grandparents' home back on the reserve.

The only difference there was that we all sat at the same huge dining room table. There was room enough for at least sixteen people, and my aunt had her own spot set up in the kitchen so she could oversee everything happening at the main table. Whenever something ran low, she would refill the item from her assortment of huge cooking pots. My aunt took immense pride in how well she took care of everyone in attendance.

There was always enough food prepared, along with a little extra just in case someone should happen to show up late. Mealtimes were special at my grandparents' home. They did not like to see anyone go hungry. This was something I noticed in every First Nations home.

My mother, like most other women trying to raise a family on the reservation, had a large vegetable garden, and it was planted next to the house to keep the wildlife and the neighbourhood kids from destroying it. There was always some form of wild game our relatives or neighbours brought by, so we ate well considering everyone else in the local town thought of us as "those poor little Indian kids from the reservation."

As children we were surrounded by family members who did their best to ensure there was enough food on the table to keep us alive and content. To us this was everyday life. Maybe it was not much in the eyes of white society, or the big shots who ran the Department of Indian and Northern Affairs in Ottawa, but it was all any of us had ever known in our young lifetimes, and it was ours.

As the long, hot summer months slowly came to an end, my friends and I happily enjoyed ourselves, frolicking in the afternoon sun. We did our best to spend as many daylight hours as possible enjoying the cool, refreshing water of the small lake just a short walk from where we lived. All the local kids saw it as our own personal beach, just like the white people had down in the nearby valley. Ours was known as Sunset Beach.

We may not have had much, but at that point in my young life I did not think of us as being poor or underprivileged. The most important things in our lives were that we were happy, fed, and had a roof over our heads. As far as we were concerned, life on the reserve was good.

Little did I know that as that summer came to an end, so too would the happy, jubilant, and carefree days I had come to know. No longer would I be able to run as fast as I could across the wide-open prairie in front of our small blue and white house, chasing old tires or homemade arrows with my siblings and childhood friends from the area. No more of the simple things, like enjoying the fragrant smells from the varieties of wildflowers and buffalo sage that blanketed the prairie landscape around our community.

No more of those wonderfully lazy days spent splashing in the lake with my friends as we tried our best to beat the heat from the hot afternoon sun. Instead, I would end up spending the next eleven years amongst strangers who made it their mission to take the Indian out of the boy at any cost, something that was mandated by the government.

Right from the start they subjected me to all the same old and too-familiar rituals that you will hear spoken repeatedly from practically everyone who was put through their awful school system. First, my long, dark hair was buzz-cut almost to the scalp, and I was repeatedly washed with delousing liquid. All this even though most of us had never had lice, or any of the other kinds of bugs that they were all so afraid of catching from us. Our parents always made sure of it.

This would be followed up with a scentless white powder applied to everyone's head at least once a month. I was dressed in new clothes and a shiny new pair of cheap dress shoes that were meant to keep everyone looking alike. These outfits helped everyone distinguish us as school property. We were also given one nice set of clothes that were only to be worn for Sunday Mass, or any of their other special Catholic celebrations, such as baptisms, first communions, Christmas Mass, Easter Mass, and so on.

Even after the years that have passed, I can recall my first day in that awful school as though it was yesterday. In the beginning everything seemed okay, because just like any other small child from anywhere in the world, I enjoyed being given the opportunity to spend the day playing with a bunch of new friends, most of whom I had never seen before. We were just a group of young children enjoying each other's company without any of the usual prejudices that divide everyone else.

However, as the long day came to an end and I found myself growing increasingly tired, I wanted to go home. This is when the harsh reality of my situation became clear, and I found out that I was not allowed to leave. I could hardly believe what was happening to me, because never in my young life had I been forced to do something I did not want to do. This was foreign to me, and I hated it.

As I sat there crying on a long wooden bench in the middle of the large playroom, the supervisor laughed and yelled at me hatefully. He told me the only reason I was there was because my family no longer wanted anything to do with me. He told me that I now belonged to them, and they could do whatever they wanted with me. I cried myself to sleep on that hard bench with his cruel words ringing loudly in my ears.

For the longest time I believed what he had said, and I would ask myself, "What did I do that was so bad that my own family don't want me anymore?" For the next few years, I cried myself to sleep at night believing I was being punished for something I had done and wondering if I would ever be forgiven for my wrongdoing so I could go home, back to the small house on the hill just above the lake, the place I dreamt about every night once the crying was finally over.

From that day forward, I was no different than anyone else at the school. We were treated like nothing more than government property and referred to by numbers rather than our given names. When we were home on the reserve, we had personal band-status numbers, used to identify us when we required anything in the way of education or health matters. These status cards, as they are referred to, have become the primary form of identification for anyone of First Nations descent, whether they resided on the reserve or not. These new numbers issued to us by the school were no different.

As soon as one of us found ourselves in one of these residential schools, we were issued with a number we had to use whenever we wanted anything. When we picked up our clean clothes from the school laundry room, they did not ask us for our name, they asked us for our number. It was clearly marked on small white tags on the inside waistband of our jeans and shorts, and on the insides of the collars on our shirts, jackets, and T-shirts, before they were issued. If this tag fell off, we had to have it replaced.

Even the bed and locker that everyone was assigned had our identification number marked on it. It was like a cattle brand so that everyone knew exactly what was theirs and where it belonged. We were told that we would find ourselves in serious trouble if we were caught wearing someone else's clothes or being in someone else's locker. We had one locker issued to us in the dormitory for our clothing and a second in the playroom area for our heavy winter boots, jackets, and sports equipment.

When I was younger and still attending my first school, at Marieval, Saskatchewan, I was given the number 27. This was mine for approximately seven years. When I was transferred to the second school in Lebret, Saskatchewan, at the age of eleven, it was changed to 74. I always hated those two numbers and how we all had to stand around in the playroom waiting for our number to be called whenever they handed something out, or when they did a quick head count to make sure that no one had wandered off or decided to run away while they were not looking, two things known to happen now and then.

We couldn't even get away from it when we were on the school playground attempting to enjoy ourselves, because they would simply holler our numbers over the screechy and awful-sounding intercom if they wanted any of us to report to a particular area. Sometimes I cannot help thinking to myself that we have all been nothing more than numbers in our own country. Just the thought of this is enough to cause feelings of anger all over again.

As a result of the residential school system, most of my life has been spent living in a state of absolute turmoil over the many extremely painful experiences and unspeakable acts that were forcibly inflicted upon so many generations of First Nations people. Sometimes it felt as though we were not even considered human beings. We were nothing more than pieces of property that the federal government could do with as they pleased. When they were happy with us, they would reward us; if they were angry, they would hold back things like money or housing-related materials.

Even today, if you go online and read about the many painful residential school experiences of our people, you can see and hear the blatant and painfully racist comments that still exist in modern-day society, a society that is considered "much improved." In fact, the government likes to say that Canada is the most racially tolerant society anywhere in the free world.

What I experienced over the eleven-year period I was forced to be there was bad enough. Adding the hundreds of stories told to me by other survivors, it was easy to understand how I became angry at and resentful of the world around me. These were emotions I carried around inside me for a vast number of years, and at no time did I ever make an attempt to hide them from anyone around me. In fact, most people knew better than to bring up the topic of residential school, especially if I had been drinking.

At one point in my life, I had nothing but absolute hatred for anyone or anything even remotely associated with the Church. As a matter of fact, people in positions of authority of any kind were looked upon with contempt and distrust, even those with jobs in no way associated with the Church or the government. I had simply learned to distrust everyone in white society around me, no matter what their occupation was.

This attitude has caused me a great deal of personal grief over the years. It became difficult to hold any kind of job in the non-Aboriginal community. I found that I could not take orders from non-Aboriginal people. I often thought that Caucasian people were trying to ridicule me or put me down simply because of who I was. Most times I would tough it out until I received my paycheque, then simply pack up and leave without saying a word to anyone.

If not for the Elders who took the time to sit me down and slowly teach me the true meaning of compassion and forgiveness, I would probably still be lost and dwelling in the negative environment of self-pity and anger, the place where I always found myself hating life and not caring about people or events around me.

A few years ago, I began seeing a psychological therapist in Vancouver who specialized in dealing with what they had begun to call "residential school trauma." She was a Métis lady who had never attended residential school, so at first, I found it hard to take her seriously. I kept asking myself how she could possibly be able to talk about the school experiences if she never experienced them for herself. It just did not seem possible.

She quickly helped me to understand that trauma is trauma regardless of whether someone went to residential school. She was the first person to tell me I had every right to be angry over what happened to me as a child. She not only helped me understand a lot about what I was feeling and why I was experiencing these emotions, but with her help I learned how to accept all these feelings, and I found myself slowly beginning to move forward in a healthy and positive manner.

Along with everything else that my Elders have taught me over the years, this psychologist helped me realize that it does not matter what other people think about me, because I will never be able to please everyone at the same time, no matter how hard I am willing to try. They both taught me that the most important thing in life is what I think of myself, and how I choose to portray myself to the rest of the world. What other people choose to see in me is something they must live with.

My therapist also told me I had an important choice to make regarding my future: I could continue to view myself as a person unworthy of anything in life, or I could begin to see myself as someone with as much right to success and happiness as everyone else in the world. Whatever decision I made, the important thing I had to remember was that it was *my* choice, and always had been. No one else had this power over me.

She taught me not to be ashamed of my past. She pointed out that none of us can change what has already been done, no matter how hard we try. We could all throw ourselves on the ground, kicking and screaming, but when all is said and done, nothing will have changed. In fact, we will find that our situation has worsened because of our foolish actions.

She told me I had to accept that the past is all a part of who I am today, and I must learn to accept it for what it is. She explained how everything I have experienced getting to this point in my life has helped me to define the person I have evolved into as an adult survivor. These negative experiences have shaped who I am and are the main reason I found the strength to stand up for myself and tell the rest of the world, "I am still here, despite what you have thrown at me."

She said the best thing any of us can do for ourselves, and for the world around us, is look closely at what got us to the current point in our lives and learn from our mistakes so we can move forward in a healthy and positive way without repeating any of them. This is why a lot of survivors like me go in and out of jail.

Surprisingly, this psychologist's words are no different than any of the teachings I have received from the many Elders I have been lucky enough to work with over the past twenty years. This is why I say I view many of our First Nations Elders as our people's first psychologists and therapists. Most people understand and agree with me once we sit and think about it together for a while.

They do the same job that highly trained professionals do. They not only teach, but they also listen and counsel individuals to help them through problems in a positive manner, one that is beneficial to everyone concerned. They may not always get the same recognition as the highly paid psychologists, but their teachings and guidance are just as effective and beneficial to the people they serve in their various communities across what we have always known as Turtle Island.

Several Elders from different areas of Turtle Island share similar teachings about learning to live with our pasts. Often, we as First Nations people foolishly allow our personal histories to prevent us from moving forward and going after something that we want in life, like good jobs or associates, both business and personal. We are all too quick to bow our heads and walk away rather than stand up for something we have every right to.

Instead of going after something we have dreamt about for most of our lives, we will often discourage ourselves by using that same old negative self-talk. We convince ourselves that others won't like us anyway, because of who we are or because of our pasts, even though they haven't got a clue who we are. We assume that everyone else in the world has us all figured out.

One Elder told me that we all need to understand one simple rule: our pasts do not define who we are, they are just made up of events that have helped us grow into the people we are today. He said that if a man steals a bike when he is twelve, he does not have to be known for the rest of his life as the bicycle thief.

We all must recognize these things as learning curves that help us grow into positive human beings by teaching us not to repeat the same mistakes later in life. He told me that there is no one on earth who can say that they have never made a mistake. Not even the Pope himself can make such a claim.

Despite all the healing I have done over the past thirty years, I still find it difficult to believe that I survived eleven years of my childhood in a place so dark and cruel, being punished and humiliated daily simply for having been born a First Nations child.

My childhood in those residential schools was like walking on eggshells. I tried hard not to be noticed for fear of becoming the next one forced to face the wrath of some angry supervisor, or one of the older students, who could often be just as cruel to the younger kids. These older kids seemed to feed off the supervisors, treating the younger children the same way. They actually thought that it was okay.

I lived every day in shame, constantly being called a pagan or a filthy savage by the very people who were supposed to be educating me. I do not know how any of us were supposed to learn anything in class when we were too afraid of the teacher to ask questions, even when we did not understand what was expected of us. These were the classes run by teachers who had a reputation for hitting students, either with a book or a yardstick. They did not talk to us; they yelled and screamed at us daily.

Whenever someone was foolish enough to speak about home on the reserve, they were ridiculed for it immediately and told they should forget about it, because all they had to look forward to there was a life of alcohol and welfare, just like the rest of their family. I heard those words on more than one occasion, from different teachers.

They assumed everyone living on the reserves were lazy, unemployed alcoholics, which was far from the truth. There were plenty of people living out there I never saw touch a drop of alcohol for as long as I had known them. Sure, there was alcohol around from time to time, but it was not like people drank every day from sunup till sundown. They had lives with routines like everyone else.

When they did go out, someone always made sure we were fed and taken care of before they left. And as for that meagre amount of welfare provided to most families, the government wanted us to be dependent on them and their small monthly handouts, just as long as we were obedient and quiet. That is how all the federal government's Indian reserves were designed to be run: they were simply meant to keep everyone in one place and as subordinate as possible. This applies even in today's so-called modern society.

Still, there was always someone available at the school more than willing to remind us of just how useless we were, and to tell us we would never amount to anything in life. Sometimes one of the nuns would take pride in reminding us we could not get into heaven, simply because we were born into an Aboriginal community.

They would wave a finger at us while saying that the closest we could ever get to heaven was *purgatory*, where we were all going to burn for *eternity*. This was our punishment from their god for being born First Nations people—even though he was the one who chose to make us into the people that we were.

It was all so confusing, because one minute they would tell us what a wonderful and kind individual their god is and how he always forgives your sins if you ask him, then they would tell us about how he was going to throw us all into a lake of fire and ash. I never knew what to believe. I would wonder to myself, *if there really is a god, why does he allow us to be treated like this?* Didn't he hear our prayers too? Were our prayers somehow different?

I was never sure whether I was supposed to love their god and look up to him or fear him for what he might do to me in anger. They would tell us that all of humankind was born with a black mark on our souls because of what Adam and Eve did to get themselves kicked out of the Garden of Eden. They would proceed to tell us all about how this mark could only be washed away if we were baptized by their church and given *Confirmation*, so that we could receive the *Holy Communion* when we went to church for Sunday Mass.

However, we were told that as Indian children we were also seen as pagans, which meant that we all carried a second mark that was almost impossible to remove. I often wondered, since we were so different from everyone else, why we carried that first mark because of what Adam and Eve did if they were not even Indian. As far as I was concerned, this should have been the white man's problem, not ours. None of this made any sense to me at all.

These were the types of teachings that were responsible for the hatred and distrust that I developed toward their god and his church over the years. I was quick to remind myself that there was no way I wanted to go to their heaven anyway, because I would be forced to put up with those people all over again. It was a difficult situation.

As for this individual that they referred to as *the devil*, I thought he could not possibly be any worse than they were. I had seen every kind of evil there was, and it was all right here on earth. I lived with it daily.

Aside from the beatings that many of us would receive for speaking our own languages, or having our mouths washed out with soap for talking about the ceremonial practices deemed to be nothing more than devil worship by these so-called representatives of God, we now had to put up with years of having their religious beliefs forced upon us.

I could not for the life of me understand why they were so against us speaking our own language when they were trying so hard to teach us how to speak in theirs, which was French. As a child of five, all of this can be scary and overwhelming. Sometimes when one of the Catholic nuns became frustrated or angry with us, they would holler in French, which added to the confusion.

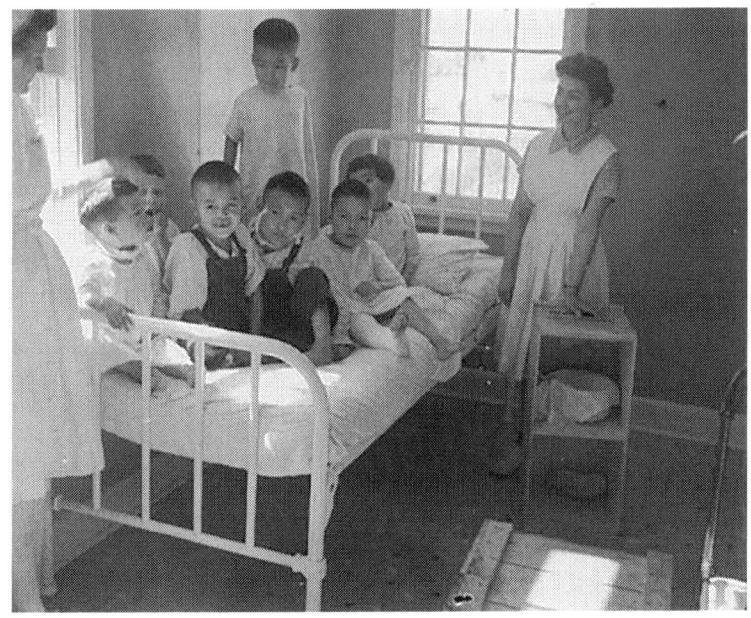

Children as young as four and five years old were taken, as is apparent from this photo.

Chapter 2

It is important to remember that as young children our primary caregivers in life are considered to be our first and most important teachers. They shape and mould us into the individuals we become. They play a significant role in our level of standards and beliefs. Under normal circumstances, this role would be filled by our parents and grandparents, who shared the task of raising us within the circle that makes up the Seven Sacred Teachings that Native spirituality is based upon. They are like our version of the Ten Commandments.

The residential school system broke that sacred circle and left us without these teachers to provide us with two of the most important teachings: love and compassion. I have often heard it said over the past few years that the basic human need in life is to love and to be loved. When that is taken away from you as a child it leaves a big void in the most important years of your personal development, something you can never fully regain despite years of trying to relearn it as an adult.

Thanks to what the Elders have taught me over the past thirty years, as well as the psychological help that I have been given from my therapist, I am slowly learning to forgive, and see things in a new light. I am also now able to accept the sad reality that some of the people responsible for the horrific abuse inflicted upon so many First Nations children were themselves unhealthy and in need of help. I have been able to accept that the world live in is not a perfect place, and human beings are by no means a perfect race.

People have forgotten how to show compassion toward one another and the world around them. We need to focus on the good in others, rather than only the bad. As long as we refuse to accept this, things will continue to get worse, not only for Aboriginal people, but for humanity. These are the teachings that our Elders have been trying so hard to share with the world for the past three hundred years, but no one will listen to them or take them seriously.

Most residential school survivors will tell you how they rarely witnessed or received even the smallest forms of compassion while they attended those awful schools. The only sincere examples of comfort and understanding they received came from other children of their own age who knew what they were going through, because they had to live through it as well. They understood your pain.

Most survivors who are willing to speak openly will tell you that during their childhood they hardly ever experienced something as simple as a caring hand placed on their shoulder to say *good job*, or *well done*. We never had anyone there to hug us and help us dry our tears when we were experiencing pain or discomfort. They would often just yell at us to stop the damn crying and act like an adult. The problem was that we were not adults, we were children.

Unfortunately, countless numbers of our First Nations children from all over Turtle Island, myself included, have grown up without hearing someone say, "I love you." Most survivors have never received any of the love and nurturing that is usually provided by parents and grandparents in a healthy and loving environment. Instead, we grew up learning that *love* was a dirty word.

That is why so many of our people today have difficulty dealing with that type of emotion now that we are living in our adult years. It has been said that as human beings we will have done most of our learning about who we are and what values we will follow in life by the time we are eight. This is according to all the so-called leading experts in child development and learning, experts who have gone through some of the world's most well-respected institutions of knowledge and learning. These are people with every kind of degree imaginable.

Therefore, because we as survivors were never shown love or compassion while growing up in church-run schools, we in turn did not know how express love and affection to our own family members. As we all began being considered adult enough to begin teaching and passing things on to our own children, we were lost and had no idea what we were supposed to be doing.

As a teacher, you can only pass on what you have been shown by those who raised you. When you are never allowed to experience any form of compassion, how can you be expected to pass that kind of emotion on to your own children and grandchildren? Most of the time I was only capable of showing other people the same cold emotions shown to me as a child. I had no idea how to be compassionate toward another person.

When it came time for me to become a parent and raise my own children, I was once again lost. I did my best to protect them and see to it they had clean clothes and food, but when it came to teaching and providing them with the loving and nurturing those other children received, I was a failure. I understood why my mother was considered a poor parent: she went through the same residential school system I did.

Sure, I hugged my children whenever they were sad and fed them when they were hungry and carried them around when they cried or could not sleep, but I had no idea how to provide the proper love and compassion that they needed and deserved. Nobody showed me or took the time to explain how to be a good parent, and children do not come with instruction manuals.

Despite never having these things growing up, I knew I had to find a way of providing them for my children.

I was only able to guess at things most of the time and then try to do whatever I thought was right. Often, I would remember something I saw on television or read in a book. It was all "live and learn," but at least it was better than what I received as a child. Luckily, I had an older sister who had already raised four children of her own, so I was able to ask her for advice from time to time. Even though she too became a residential school survivor, she at least had firsthand experience, and she was more than happy to share it with me.

When my children were infants, I would often look at them sleeping peacefully and want to break down crying. I had no idea what I was doing, and I knew that they deserved something better out of life than what I was capable of providing. The only thing that I was certain about was that I did not want them to go through the awful childhood that had been inflicted on me. There was no way that I would willingly allow my children to be placed in one of those awful schools.

Deep inside I was aware that they were solely my responsibility, and that scared the heck out of me. I spoke to one of my closest friends about all of this, who was lucky enough to have never been through residential school. He laughed and told me that kids were not particularly complicated; all that really mattered was that they were happy and content. He told me that all First Nations children have a wonderful way of adapting to their surroundings and surviving. It was just human nature—didn't those schools prove that?

Being a product of the residential school system had unwittingly caused me to walk around for years in a daze. Not only did I lack the knowledge to be a proper parent or to show love and compassion, but I also knew nothing about the grieving process or the dangers that come from not dealing with grief in a proper and timely manner. Like most survivors, I kept the pain and anger inside, which ultimately opened the door to substance abuse as a means of coping.

I had never dealt with the things I had lost to my time in the residential school system, I had simply learned how to keep it bottled up. Not dealing with any of these losses affected me negatively, but I could not seem to notice any of this until after I had seen a trauma therapist for well over a year. Until she began pointing things out to me, I went on believing my life was perfectly normal.

Until I worked with the therapist, I did not know that by not grieving properly I was risking my health and sanity, as well as the wellbeing of those around me. I had no way of knowing that all of this could lead to suicide and addiction, two of the common problems amongst survivors and their families.

Therefore, we keep hearing about suicide epidemics in remote First Nations communities, particularly among the youth who have no one to teach them about the dangers associated with the residential school legacy. Most of these young people are the children or grandchildren of survivors like me.

I learned at an incredibly early age not to cry or let my emotions show, because I was putting myself at risk of being ridiculed or humiliated again. Now that I was finally an adult, I did not know how to deal with grief. All I knew how to do was reach for the nearest bottle or drug. This became my way of coping with any emotion I could not understand or control. I often tell people that it felt like I had no centre, which in turn caused me to feel as though I did not belong. No matter where I went or how far I ran, it was always the same. The feeling never left.

This state of constant confusion caused me to turn to substance abuse as a way of coping, just like so many survivors before me had done. I cannot speak for them, but I know that this was *my* way of coping with the pain I was trying so desperately to run from. Whenever I just could not handle it any longer, I would do my best to drown out the memories the only way I knew how. It was temporary, but at least the pain along with all the awful memories were gone for a while. At least until I sobered up.

Unlike all the so-called "normal" people, I did not go out to party. I went out with the sole purpose of hitting the blackout stage as quickly as possible, because I wanted to numb the pain I was carrying deep inside. I believed that no living person could ever be able to understand what I was going through on the inside. Something told me that people would laugh or consider me weak if I tried explaining to them what I was feeling.

I was worried that people would consider some of my behaviours extraordinary or foolish. When I was in my twenties, I realized I couldn't look people directly in the eyes when I was speaking to them, except when I was trying to intimidate them. No matter how hard I tried to overcome this affliction, I could not stop myself from looking down or away whenever I was talking to a non-Aboriginal, no matter who they were or how long I had known them. This had been engrained in me from childhood.

People were constantly pointing this out to me and telling me that I really needed to work on it, because it led everyone to believe that I was hiding something from them, or that I was not telling the truth. Most of the residential school survivors I have met over the years suffer from similar conditions, which can be traced back to their childhood and are often a result of a traumatic experience they witnessed or suffered.

I was slapped across the face, hard, on more than one occasion for looking someone in the eye while they were reprimanding me for something I had done or something I was believed to have done. They would holler something directly in my face like, "How dare you challenge me?" or "Keep your eyes on the floor!" Sometimes we would refuse to look down out of spite, even though we knew they would get angrier and begin to hit us harder.

Before it was all over, we would end up standing in the corner of the room with our noses pressed firmly into it. Often, we would then remain there for the next few hours until they were done tormenting us. Only then would they return to holler at us a few more times before telling us to get out of their sight, which we gladly did.

As a small child I learned that looking an adult in the eyes would get me into serious trouble. Today I find this habit difficult to deal with, because I want people to know that I am speaking to them straight from the heart. I do not want them thinking that I am intentionally lying to them or keeping them in the dark about something.

My therapist explained to me that when they made us keep our eyes down while talking to them, it was another way of teaching us to be submissive. It was just one more sick way they exerted dominance over a group of defenceless children. This behaviour even made some of the perpetrators excited. That is why they did not want you to look them in the face—they were afraid you would see them for who they really were.

When I tell non-Native people about my experiences, they often say, "Come on now, it couldn't have been all that bad." Then they add, "After all, it was just a school." Some people have told me they thought going away to a boarding school sounded like a fun experience. They thought that it was no different than going away to summer camp for a while or having a sleepover with friends. They said they would look at the experience as a chance to get away from their family for a while and not have to worry about cleaning their room or making their bed.

I tell them those were the same things they made us do every day, except there was usually a nun standing over us with a cold, stern look on her face, watching our every move. If we did not do things to her satisfaction, she would simply rip the bed apart and make us start over again until she felt satisfied with the way we had completed the task. There were no maids in residential school either, so guess who had to do all the house cleaning? Remember that these were exceptionally large schools, often three or four stories high.

I would tell people stories about how we were always hungry, and how some children would hide pieces of bread or fruit for later in the evening. They did this because they knew they were going to be hungry again right before bedtime. These poor children would be severely punished for doing this if they were caught. Some of them were not even doing it for themselves, they were looking out for a younger sibling or another child who was all alone with no one to look out for their wellbeing. There were so many of them in these schools.

There were countless times I had to listen to little kids crying at night because they were hungry or lonesome. Most of the time there was nothing any of us could do except try to comfort the child by talking with them as we waited for morning to arrive. If we were lucky, they would fall asleep well before that time, which would allow us to get some sleep as well. I tell people that I know all of this to be true because I often hid food for the smaller ones and was punished on more than one occasion for doing so. Even today I cannot stand to see anyone go hungry.

There were also the European holidays, like Easter, Halloween, Christmas, and Thanksgiving, when the staff celebrated while we were forced to sit back and watch. Carts with fancy foods and baked goods were pushed through our dining room into the staff's private dining area, and they would feast on the best of everything while we ate our usual bland meals, which were evenly measured and weighed by the kitchen staff.

When one of us was caught looking up at the cart with all the fancy cakes and cookies we were immediately scolded by one of the nuns and told to mind our own plates. Sometimes we were blessed enough to receive a cookie or a small piece of cake, but most of the time we were lucky if we got a piece of fruit. I hated the fact that they would sit in their private dining area and eat like royalty while we always went to bed hungry.

The only times we received special meals was when someone from Ottawa or a high-ranking Church official like the bishop showed up. Then they would put away the ugly plastic trays we normally ate off and break out the fine China. The children would be dressed in our finest clothes and paraded around for the visitors to see. This was one of the few times other than Sunday Mass when we got to wear our good clothes without being punished for it.

Most of the time we did not know who these people were, but we knew they were important from the way everyone scurried around seeing to their every need and trying to make them as comfortable as possible. The only thing any of us understood was that when these people came to visit, we would get to experience what it was like to eat the fancy food that the staff usually ate in their private dining room. Even as small children we knew it was just a big show for the visiting officials, but we made the best of it and enjoyed ourselves, at least for that day.

There was also the annual Christmas pageant, put on in the big community hall every year for the same officials and their families. Some of us would end up dressed as some form of farm animal and made to stand around in front of a plastic doll that represented their baby Jesus in a manger filled with straw. We would have to stand there for hours in hot and itchy costumes listening to one of the teachers repeat that same story about the three wise men and their gifts.

When she was finally finished, we would all have to sing dreadful songs that meant nothing to us. By this time, I was about ready to scream or go sleep in a corner. I hated this part of the show, but I knew that when things were winding down, we would be called up to the stage one at a time so we could receive a gift from the Church, usually new socks, and mittens. Along with these we would receive a small bag of candy and a few mandarin oranges provided by the visitors from the school's head office or the Church.

Some of the smaller children appeared to enjoy these events. I saw it as another opportunity to get out of the classroom for the day, and it was something different from the usual routine we had all become accustomed to. Some of the kids did their best to eat all their candy before someone took the opportunity to take it back, while others quietly hid it away for later.

For most of the kids, this would be the only sweets they would see for the year, so it was easy to understand why they behaved that way, when something they rarely saw was suddenly placed in their hands. Although the school supervisors operated a small canteen in the corner of the playroom, not everyone was fortunate enough to have family members visit them on the weekends and leave them a few dollars to spend on treats.

Most of the children never saw anyone from home for years because they lived so far away. All these children had was each other, and the school had become their world. I was lucky if I saw my family once or twice a year. Most times I went home with someone else.

Whenever I would begin telling non-Native people about the hunger or abuses that regularly occurred in these government-run schools, they would tell me how difficult they found it to believe that anything like this would occur in this country. Most of these people refused to believe that any of the churches would allow anything like this to happen. The Catholic people I met would always tell me that the Pope would never stand for anything like this, because it not only goes against everything that the Bible stands for, but it is also just plain inhumane.

They would tell me this sort of thing only happens in developing countries, not here in what they have all grown to know as the "free world." Sometimes when I finally catch myself becoming frustrated with these people and their ignorance, I ask them if they have ever been to a reservation anywhere in their so-called free world. Some of them gasp and give me a look that says, *are you kidding me? What makes you think that I would even consider going to one of those awful places?*

Most of these people have not passed through an actual reservation, let alone taken the time to stop and visit one. When I tell them that the majority of these reservations are about as developing an area as you can get, they give me a blank look of confusion and disbelief. To them Canada is as far away from a developing nation as the moon. They just cannot accept this idea.

They all grew up believing that First Nations people had it made living on these reservations. They were led to believe that everything was provided to us at the taxpayers' expense. Most of them heard we all received free housing and medical care along with those great educations their government was providing to us. I wish I could take them all out to visit some of these reserves for just one hour, the ones that are farther away from the city and are not in any way influenced by what is happening in the urban environment.

Then there are those who have actually been to one of the local reserves situated in the heart of a city like Vancouver. These individuals may have visited one of these communities for a sporting event, or even for one of the many smalls Pow-wows that occur within the city limits each year. These are the only reserves that they have ever seen, so naturally they believe that all other reservations across the country are the same.

When I tell them that these are what are known as "urban reserves," ones that look no different than the rest of the city so they cannot really be compared to an actual reservation, they are amazed. This is when I like to show them pictures from places like Pine Ridge, South Dakota, the site of the Wounded Knee massacre, and many cannot believe the difference. One of the people I showed these pictures to thought I was trying to fool him by showing him pictures from South America or Mexico.

I cannot blame these non-Native people for not knowing what goes on at the reserve level, because no one has ever told them anything. Even in their public-school curriculum, there is no factual information about the history surrounding the First

Nations people, even though this is our home country. The only teachings I can recall hearing about in our social studies classes were about how the Huron, Algonquin, and Iroquois people helped create the fur trade business in Eastern Canada.

There were also numerous stories about how Captain Cook supposedly discovered and tamed the entire West Coast. Considering the lack of knowledge regarding most of the original inhabitants of this country, I can understand the ignorance that most non-Native people have regarding the Indigenous people and their ongoing struggles, even though many of these struggles have been going on for close to five hundred years.

Most non-Aboriginal people in this country still refuse to believe that, while implementing the residential schools, our government not only developed a policy designed to take "the Indian out of the child at any cost," but they put it into law. This is still documented in the government's archives in Ottawa and is something they only reluctantly admitted to during the recent Truth and Reconciliation process. The government does not like this type of truth to be told under normal circumstances; therefore, this is not something that is taught in the history books of our great country.

Back when they signed this document into effect, it was their goal to strategically eliminate all signs of our culture, including spiritual practices and what they considered to be paganistic beliefs. They said they needed to eradicate the country of the Indians by turning them into proper Christian people. Those who refused to convert to Christian beliefs were annihilated.

They believed the easiest way to accomplish all of this was to break up the family circle and remove all the children from their communities so they could teach them to think and live like average white citizens. When you try to tell people that this kind of behaviour meets all the UN's definitions for cultural genocide, most will become defensive and walk away, shaking their heads in a state of disgust or anger.

I like to point out to these people that the first step of any oppressor is to systematically break down the cultural and spiritual values of the group or community they are going after, replacing them with the values of the dominant group, because values are what tie any community together. Once this has been done, they will remove all the children, the future of the society they are trying to conquer or change. They know that by systematically breaking the family circle they will strike at the very core of the community they are going after.

The federal government knew exactly what it was doing when it implemented those laws prohibiting our cultural and spiritual activities. They deliberately forced the children into Church-run residential schools to be brainwashed and reprogrammed into believing the non-Native society was better than their own. The sad part is that the federal government believed that what it was doing was in the best interests of the First Nations people, an attitude that has not changed to this day.

A lot of these non-Native people become angry when I tell them that Canada was, and still is, one of the most racist countries in the world. There is systemic racism in every major corporation or organization in this country. It exists in health care, schools, prisons, police forces, the military, no matter where you look, it rears its ugly head. I like to point out how I can recall Canada being one of four countries out of 148 in the United Nations Assembly that refused to consider or sign UNDRIP: the United Nations Declaration on the Rights of Indigenous Peoples.

I tell them to look at the more than 1,200 missing and murdered Aboriginal women and the Canadian government's racist views regarding them. Then there is the Conservative Party's Minister of Indian Affairs who stated on national television that it was Aboriginal men who were mostly responsible for these deaths. He stated that it was simply because First Nations women were not given any real rights or protection on their own reservations that they were open to abuse of every kind. He neglected to say that it was their federal government that was responsible for implementing the Indian Act, which dictates the rules on all the reservations in Canada.

Whenever I hear one of the government's own officials making this kind of ignorant statement, the only thing I can think to say is that these words are spoken by a true politician. Part of me wants to tell them they should start by first honouring the treaties their predecessors signed before they start pointing fingers. After all, we aren't the ones who created the rules that reserves are run by, so how can these people now turn around and point the fingers at us? It seems to me that the Department of Indian and Northern Affairs, as well as the Indian Act, is still run by the people in Ottawa.

Somehow Canada always seems to be the first country to point its finger at another when it comes to human rights violations, but they make no effort to clean up their own backyard. The late Nelson Mandela said that apartheid is apartheid no matter where it is happening. He compared the treatment of Aboriginal people here in Canada to what he saw back home in his country of South Africa, and he said that he saw no difference between the two countries when it came to oppressing the people. The dominant white society was trying to oppress the original inhabitants and exert its authority over the lands they had stolen.

Most people today do not understand how deep the scarring from the residential school experience has affected the First Nations community. Families were torn apart and not permitted to associate with each other for years. I have siblings I have not seen in over fifty years because of this policy. I remember seeing parents show up at the school on weekends to try to visit with their children, only to be turned away and told that the children were not available for one reason or another. Even while attending the same school, brothers and sisters were not allowed to mingle with each other. When they were allowed to see each other in class or at a school *function*, there were usually one or two nuns there to ensure they did not hug each other or show any form of compassion or affection. This was strictly against the rules of all the schools and strongly enforced.

All forms of physical contact between boys and girls were forbidden within the confines of the school's property. We were all taught that "love" was a dirty word, never to be spoken. As a result, most First Nation family members have failed to bond with each other in a proper manner, like so-called *normal* families. This kind of inhumane brainwashing has negative effects on our people many generations later.

It has left entire families broken and unable to come together to lend support to one another, even in the most critical of times such as sickness or death. Problems associated with these dysfunctional families can be witnessed in any First Nations community you visit. Some survivors still do not like to be hugged or touched, even by their own family members. This is all part of the residential school legacy.

Whenever I am out and hear groups of young people talking in one of the local malls or restaurants about how wonderful their high school years were, or how much they are looking forward to their graduate, I smile and try to imagine what that must be like. I realize people are supposed to be able to look back at their academic years with fond memories, talk about childhood pranks, and think of the wonderful friendships they hope will last a lifetime. However, none of this applies to us as survivors.

For those of us who attended residential school, all of that is just a dream, the stuff that Hollywood movies are made of. We grew up in a scary place where the bogeyman was the person most often in charge of your day-to-day life. He was always there watching and waiting for you to let your guard down, or to make one small mistake so that he could pounce on you. Like most survivors I did my best to forget my academic years; they were not something that I wanted to remember or reflect on.

During the many years I spent on the Black Road, as I have now come to call it, I refused to allow anyone to get too close to me. Sure, I had my share of relationships, just like everyone else, but I never gave myself totally to any of my partners. Truth be known, I really did not know how to be a good partner. I always gave just enough of myself to keep the relationship going, but always managed to keep my partner at arm's length. This was what those schools taught me.

I can't remember ever saying "I love you" to anyone unless I was under the influence of drugs or alcohol. Sure, I loved people, but I did not know how to show it, or even how to say it. If someone did manage to get too close, I found a way to break off the relationship. I became quite good at that.

When someone treated me too well, I honestly did not know how to react, so I simply ran. This practice was a result of the things I had learned as a child growing up in residential school. Years of abuse left me with a dysfunctional lifestyle that unwittingly affected everyone who encountered me, including my own loved ones.

One of the many Christian ceremonies we were forced to participate in. This is the Confirmation ceremony so the children could have Communion at Sunday Mass.

The old school at Muskowekwan First Nation in Saskatchewan that was given National Historic Site status.

Chapter 3

The first residential school I attended was the Marieval Indian Residential School, often referred to as the old mission school. It was situated in the southern part of Saskatchewan, which is prime farming country. On more than one occasion being loaded into the back of a large farm truck with wooden sides, not unlike a large cattle truck. We were then transported to a farm a few miles across the valley from the school belonging to the family of one of the school's supervisors, a man named William "Bill" Apple.

Once we arrived at the farm, we would be taken out to one of the fields and told to gather up all the rocks and sticks. These were piled on a large stone boat pulled behind one of the family's old tractors.

None of us were paid a wage or even given a choice about whether we wanted to participate in this forced labour. This usually happened on the weekends, which meant we did not even get to enjoy it like most normal children out in the community. We were forced to participate in their work project rather than play.

With all the child labour laws that have been developed over the past few years I would like to believe this sort of incident would not be permitted in today's society. However, back in those days, we as First Nations people did not matter much to the federal government. Because of this, they did as they pleased with us.

I am referring to the 1960s, which isn't that long ago. However, up until this point we as Aboriginal people were seen as less intelligent than non-Natives and therefore incapable of taking care of ourselves. This was the primary reason we were made wards of the government and forced to live on reservations with our lives dictated to us by the shady and unscrupulous Indian Affairs agent assigned by the government to do what was best for us, whether we agreed with him or not.

During the Truth and Reconciliation process that took place from 2008 to 2015, it was released to the public that some of the residential school students were in fact used as guinea pigs in the testing of new medicines to see if they worked before releasing them to the public. At the time they did not care whether there were negative side effects, if they were only affecting the First Nations children and not their own.

Marieval was situated in the beautiful Qu'Appelle Valley on land that belongs to the Cowessess Indian Band. This just happened to be my family's home reserve and was more than likely one of the main reasons I was later transferred to the Indian School in Lebret, Saskatchewan, when I was twelve. This move placed me well over a hundred miles away from my family and the only home I had known as a child. I believe I was moved simply because they did not want me running away from school as I grew older, something that was quite common among school kids.

Truth be told, I no longer knew where anyone lived or if I would be welcomed into their homes. If left alone I more than likely would have remained where I was. At least at Marieval I knew most of the local kids, all of whom I had grown up with. This included a considerable number I was related to. At least here I had family around me, even if they were students who were caught in the same predicament as me.

When I arrived at the new school in Lebret, the first person to meet me in the front office and escort me to the boys' side was Robert Mondour, the very supervisor who had tormented me so badly at the old school. Apparently, he too had asked for a transfer and was now the new head supervisor in the Lebret school. I could not believe my bad luck.

One of the worst memories I have from my childhood years spent at Marieval was of being strapped by the school's Catholic priest, Father Nogg, for telling him that some of us were afraid to go to sleep at night because the night watchman had been touching us. Instead of doing something to protect us from this sick and perverted individual, he asked how we could dare to try to make trouble for such a good Catholic man. We could not win no matter what.

He told us we should all be ashamed of ourselves for suggesting such a terrible thing. He opened his desk drawer and brought out a huge black rubber strap that he used across the palms of our hands. I had extremely limited use of my hands for nearly a week. Some of the other boys were a little luckier than me and barely carried any sign of the awful strapping. I suppose I got it worse because I was the spokesperson of the group.

The message we received from this incident was clear: we should all learn to be quiet about things like this in the future. This was something that bothered me for years after I left the residential school system. Even into my adult years I was unable to sleep peacefully unless my bedroom door was securely locked from the inside. Sometimes this meant putting knives or another object into the doorframe. No matter where I was, this nightly ritual became a necessity. All the people who knew me could never understand why I did strange things like this, and I was never comfortable enough with any of them to be able to sit down and talk openly about it. I think that deep down a part of me was afraid of not being believed again. This caused me to put up my defences and do the best I could to live what I perceived to be a normal life.

Even as small children, we took it upon ourselves to try to protect each other from that evil night watchman. There was a group of eight of us older boys who all slept in the same corner of the dormitory, and we agreed we would take turns staying awake at night so that everyone else around us would be able to sleep in peace without having to worry about that dreadful night watchman who came around every hour to do his punch.

This worked out great, at first. But one night a few weeks later one of my friends, Raymond, caught the night watchman touching one of the newer boys and asked him what he was doing. He responded in an angry tone, saying he was checking to make sure the young boy had not wet his bed. We knew the night watchman was lying to us, because the young boy in question wasn't one of those who suffered from that awful and humiliating problem.

We continued with our nightly watch for some time, until one morning when we overheard one of the nuns telling the supervisor that the night watchman had passed away during the night in the middle of his rounds. They said he had suffered a heart attack and was found lying on the sidewalk early the next morning. Of course, we were all ecstatic, but I felt guilty for the longest time, because someone had died, and there we were all happy, thinking only that we no longer had to worry about him touching any of us at night.

Like so many of the children taken away from their homes at an early age and submitted to these indignities, I found myself wetting the bed at night. This was something I had never done when I was at home, safely tucked in my own bed and surrounded by family members.

At first, I had my face rubbed in it by the supervisor, who seemed to extract immense pleasure in doing this to everyone. When this tactic proved not to work, or when he grew tired of the routine, he began marching us down to the large playroom where we would be forced to stand in the middle of the floor with our soiled sheets draped over our heads.

After everyone else, boys *and* girls, were in the dining hall and seated for their breakfasts, he would slowly march us through the dining room in single file with our dirty sheets still draped over our heads. We had to pass through the dining hall on our way to the laundry room, so this worked out great for him. I suffered through this humiliating ritual on so many different occasions as a child that I continued to be teased about it by my friends long after I had outgrown the problem.

As I grew older, I could not help but feel hatred for those supervisors who continued to carry out this humiliation on the unsuspecting kids who arrived at the school each year. Like clockwork, they would come rushing into the dormitory early on the first morning with huge smiles on their faces. They were all eagerly looking for the next group of innocent young victims to torment. Considering they were dealing with small children, some of whom were quite young, there was never any shortage of bedwetters to keep them amused and occupied for the rest of the school year.

On one occasion I saw a group of young boys no older than I was when I arrived at the old mission school crying on the same hard wooden bench in that middle of that large, cold playroom, just as I had done when I became aware I was being forced to stay there with these strangers and would not be going home to my family for some time. I walked away quickly that day because I did not like the memories this brought back.

I wondered if the supervisor told those young boys the same terrible story about their families not wanting them anymore. Along with my younger brother Max, who arrived one year after me, we tried our best to comfort them on that first day, but I think we both knew things were only going to get worse for them from that day forward.

Now here I was, looking down at their scared little faces as they peered out from under their soiled sheets while they trembled in the middle of the playroom, the other boys snickering around them as they waited to be marched through the packed dining hall as part of the now all too familiar march of shame, we had grown far too accustomed to seeing.

I can still recall the look of terror in their eyes as they looked up at me, pleading with me to do something to help. However, as they were being prepared to be marched through the dining hall, I knew there was nothing I could do for them now. Trying to speak up for them would only cause the already excited supervisor to turn his anger toward me, and I had felt that far too many times in the past to draw attention to myself now.

In the end I kept quiet and hung my head like everyone else who was being forced to bear witness to this cruel and sadistic act. Part of me wanted to break down and cry as I was forced to look at those tiny trembling faces with huge tears running down their cheeks. I felt such hatred and anger that I could not stop myself from shaking for the longest time afterward. This feeling stuck with me for a great many years to come.

Another time I Mr. Mondour asking one of the nuns, Sister David, if she could possibly contact the hospital supply company and obtain some of the huge hospital diapers and rubber pants, they used on patients who could not get up to use the toilet on their own. These looked like regular diapers, only they were much larger—clearly meant for people much older.

Later that week, when she brought these things to the boys' dorm, she said loudly that she had a special delivery for all the babies who were still having trouble with wetting their beds. Having to wear these at night was almost as humiliating as being marched through the dining hall every morning with your soiled bedding draped over your head while everyone else stared at you and laughed loudly.

These were only a few of the many outrageously shocking, degrading, and disparaging types of treatment that contributed so deeply to most survivors having such poor self-esteem. No matter what anyone says about this matter, I know that these events do have negative effects on anyone who was forced to witness them, let alone endure them, on a day-to-day basis for years at a time.

I am willing to agree that the residential school system did not solely contribute to the way my life turned out, but it did play a significant role in everything I experienced growing up. Residential school was the main reason I became institutionalized at an early age, which taught me how to do as I was told rather than as I wanted.

Thinking back, I admit it took me several years to finally come to terms with the fact that residential school was where I was reluctantly going to be forced to survive. It took a while, but, like everyone else, I eventually found my own place in the day-to-day routine that had become our pitiful existence. I told myself that if I was going to survive in that place, I would have to learn how to fend for myself and not count on anyone else.

I was only sure of two things in life: I was now on my own and I would learn to do whatever it took to survive. As each school year slowly dragged by, I would constantly remind myself to be patient, because I would not remain a child for much longer. I told myself that I would wait, and eventually they would find out that I was too big for them to push around. I often told myself that when that day came, I would stand up for myself and they would never lay a hand on me again under any circumstance. Even if I did not win, I would at least fight back enough to make them think about whether it was worth the effort.

As the years passed, I learned how to stay out of the line of fire and avoid the anger of those who seemed ready to yell and complain about every little thing imaginable. I had learned at an early age how to play the game. Eventually people seemed to stop taking notice of me and placed their focus on someone else, which was just fine with me.

Without even realizing it I had become a follower, more commonly referred to these days as a "people-pleaser." I would try my best to do whatever was expected of me without questioning any of the motives behind it. I convinced myself that this was what made people around me happy, and if they were happy, they would not have time to waste worrying about me.

Years of trying to avoid the wrath and anger of the supervisors and other authority figures had caused me to treat everyone as though they were the same. I slowly found myself becoming withdrawn from everyone around me and learning to jump through the hoops as they were placed in front of me, rather than questioning things I disagreed with. I was holding everything inside and waiting for my chance to get even with the world one day. I had not yet realized I was not living my life for me anymore—I was living it for everyone else.

Sometimes we can spend so much time worrying about what other people are thinking that we forget about the things we want out of life. This is where I had now found myself. Before I realized it, I was an adult with no idea what I was going to do with my life. I had no plan whatsoever, and even if I did manage to come up with one, I had no idea how I would carry it out. I was so busy being a follower that I had not bothered to prepare for my own future.

All of us want so badly to fit in and be accepted by those around us. It is never pleasant to be the outsider at any point in life. We live by certain expectations that are seldom expressed openly but always felt at some level. Out of pure desperation, we secretly try to get what we want from other people by submissively living up to their expectations without letting them know what we're after, or that we are even in need.

Our constant fear of disapproval and rejection, as well as our craving for acceptance, is why we try so hard to live up to the expectations of others and feel guilty when we do not. Sadly, this is the reality of day-to-day existence for many people in our society. All we must do is sit down and look at the people around us: are these individuals really benefiting our world, or are we helping to bolster theirs?

An Elder once asked me if I thought we are who we say we are, or who people tell us we are. I thought about it for a short time and told him that, in my opinion, we could be either, depending on the situation. He laughed loudly and told me that generally all men are a combination of both. We like to pretend we are in total control of our own lives and destinies, but we still find ourselves conforming to the wishes of our superiors, either at work or in the community where we live.

Even the most successful people in the world must conform to the standards of their bosses or risk losing their job. We just have to learn when to conform and when to not allow ourselves to become followers. We must allow ourselves our own set of standards as well as our own level of dignity. This comes into play when your superior tries to tell you to do something that goes against all your principles, and especially when they sexually harass you or a fellow employee. This is when we must ask ourselves if it is worth it because no matter what happens in life, we still have the power of choice.

When I first began on my Healing Journey back in October of 1989, I took part in a Healing Circle along with approximately forty other men. At the time I was still incarcerated in Prince Albert, Saskatchewan, and wanting desperately to change my lifestyle. The circle gathered every Wednesday evening from 5:00 p.m. until 10:00 p.m. in what was known as the "Aboriginal programming" area of the institution. This was where the Elder and liaison had their offices. Most people felt comfortable there.

This went on for the next three years, and it was extremely difficult on more occasions than I care to recall. One of the Elders conducting the circle was a Lakota man I had gotten to know and respect well. He told me that healing was not something that would come easily or simply happen overnight just because it was something I wanted. However, he assured me that it was within reach if I truly wanted it and was willing to work to achieve it.

He told me there were four simple steps that I needed to follow to begin this sacred journey. After a long pause he sat back in his chair and shook his finger in the air, saying, "Yes, it is true, a lot of terrible things were done to you as a child." He told me that before I could ever really begin any kind of a healing process, I first had to accept and acknowledge this as the truth. This, he said, is necessary, because no one can fix anything in this world until they first admit it is broken.

Secondly, I had to tell myself repeatedly that none of it was my fault, because I was only a small child at the time and unable to do anything about it.

Thirdly, he told me I needed to begin reminding myself daily that I am no longer that small child, so no one can ever do anything like that to me again.

At first, I could not understand what the Elder was trying so hard to accomplish with all this talk. Then one day he sat me down and said that the main reason I was trying so hard to destroy myself with all the substance abuse was because I was punishing myself for what had happened to me as a child. I did not like hearing any of this, but it all made perfect sense when I thought about it.

He told me that this was the fourth and most important step to my healing process. I now had to learn to stop punishing myself for the things that I had no control over. Once I accepted this I could begin learning how to forgive and move on with my life in a clean and healthy manner. This was when I decided I was going to change my life, no matter how long or hard I had to work on myself. I would not allow myself to be a quitter this time.

He told me that only when a person has accomplished all of this can they truly begin to heal themselves in a safe and healthy way. He smiled and said that everything else I wanted to accomplish in life was going to come with steps of some kind, and if I really wanted to succeed at anything I must be willing to follow all of them without looking for shortcuts. This is just how life is, he said, and no matter how much we complain we will not change this fact.

He said that nothing in life comes easy. No one can begin something in the middle and achieve any real success at what they are attempting to do. That, he said, is just how life works. You get out of it exactly what you put into it and nothing more. If I really wanted to succeed in life I had to be prepared to step up and at least give it my best effort. If I failed, at least I could say I tried.

It took me a long time to accept any of what he was saying, but eventually I was able to see the wisdom in his words and began appreciating them more each day. Every morning, as I smudged and said my prayers, I would remember those four steps with a smile. As I did this, I heard his voice in the back of my mind reminding me that everything in life is a test from the Creator. But the Creator, he would say, never gives us more than we are capable of handling. The stronger you get, the more he entrusts you with.

When I first began attending those Healing Circles, I was unable to speak openly about my residential school experiences, even when I was talking to another survivor. However, after working with the Elders for a while, I, like everyone else in the group, began to slowly feel more comfortable and began speaking freely about my personal experiences. I realized that speaking about it not only made me feel better inside, but it helped others to begin opening as well.

While participating in this circle I was surprised to see for the first-time grown men showing signs of emotions they normally hid from everyone around them. Some of these men seemed on the verge of breaking down into tears as they spoke of the terrible things they experienced in their lifetimes. This was all new to me, because up until this point I had been told to hide these feelings or people would think I was weak.

The first year in that circle taught us all how to open and release all the garbage we had been carrying around with us for so many years. The second year taught us about compassion and understanding for everything around us. The third year taught us about forgiveness and respect.

I thought the second and third years were the hardest, because you had to begin with showing these things to yourself, before you could begin to openly express them to anyone else in your daily life. Learning all of this was not something that was going to be easy or accomplished overnight.

I struggled so much in the first two years because I have always found it difficult to understand the logic behind something as simple as learning to love myself before I could love anyone else, or that I could not forgive anyone until I learned how to honestly forgive myself.

I suppose that my biggest hurdle has always been learning how to honestly look deep within myself and truthfully acknowledge the many flaws that exist there, flaws I was afraid of and that I did not want anyone else knowing about, because I thought any kind of flaw would make me look weak in the eyes of my peers. This would then open the doors to ridicule.

After all, nobody likes to openly admit that they are not as perfect as they like to portray themselves to the rest of the world. Remember that my entire childhood was spent in a place where I was taught, I was worthless and would never amount to anything in life. Because of this belief I found it difficult to accept that people could ever see anything different in me. They would always see me as nothing more than a failure.

All these things were so deeply embedded into my subconscious that I now found it extremely difficult to openly share the fact that I am not the perfect individual I portrayed. I did not want anyone knowing what any of my weaknesses were, because I had come to believe that this would open me to their ridicule and abuse.

Today when I look back at that side of my life I can laugh, because over the years I have come to understand that no human being is perfect. Everyone, no matter who they are or what culture they come from, have small things they dislike about themselves, things they often try to hide, cover up, or disguise from the rest of the world. Usually these are just foolish things that other people wouldn't care about at all. Still, the person trying to hide the incident thinks it will ruin their lives if the rest of the world found out.

An Elder once told me to remember that the only perfect ones are on the other side, and maybe one day if we prove ourselves here on earth, we too can join them in that wonderful place we often refer to as the "Spirit World." He smiled at me and said, "Yes, that place is very real." He taught me that an important part of healing is acceptance and remembering that whatever we are given in life is a gift from the Creator. We can accept and use that gift with gratitude, or we can squander it. No matter what we do, the choice is ours.

I was lucky enough to have Elders and spiritual advisors involved in my life who would not allow me to give up or feel sorry for myself, even for the shortest time. If I found myself beginning to feel down, or suddenly dwelling in self-pity, one of them would have a way of pulling me out of it.

They would usually say something as simple as, "Come on, let's go for a walk and enjoy this beautiful day." As we walked, they would tell me about all the sick people in this world who are stuck in hospital beds, unable to get up and leave their problems behind. Think about these people, they would tell me, then ask yourself if your problems are really as important as you think. Most times we find we are doing better than we thought, and that our problems are not worth talking about.

Finally, they would tell me to remember that no matter how terrible things might seem at any given moment, things could always be worse. When we think we have it bad, we should learn to stop and look around us, and we will see there are people who have it much worse than we do. We must learn how to be grateful for the things we have been provided with in life, never mind only focusing on the things we do not have.

Early into my Healing Journey, one of my biggest struggles was with what other people thought of me. It bothered me when I thought someone was mad at me or did not like me for whatever reason. When I first told this to the Elder, he smiled, poured himself a cup of coffee, and sat back in his chair. I could tell he was deep in thought by the way he smiled.

As he slowly sipped his coffee, he looked up at me in a puzzled way and said, "Just imagine for a minute how boring your life would become if everyone liked you. It would have no challenges and everything you wanted would come much too easily, because everyone would just give you everything without question." Then he said something that struck home with me: "You would have no one to pray for either."

With that, our conversation was over, and he returned to his newspaper. This was one of the things I truly admired about him: he always went straight to the point and never wasted words. There was never anything to question because I always knew exactly what he was saying. As I left his office, the only thing I could do was smile and accept what he said as coming straight from the heart.

I really enjoyed those gatherings every Wednesday night, not just because it gave us all something to do, but because it taught us the importance of solidarity and unity. We learned how to become a community again and how to look out for each other, rather than focusing on our personal needs. This thinking was extraordinary because we were in a federal maximum-security penitentiary. People in places like this generally look out for themselves and try not to pay any attention to what anyone else is doing. This is all part of the con way of thinking.

Right from the start our Elder made a point of emphasizing that a circle is like a chain: it is only as strong as its weakest link. He told us that walking the Red Road was not going to be easy for any of us, and there will be far more challenges thrown at us than anyone can handle on their own. This is why he insisted we always watch out for one another.

When you see a brother who is about to slip or do something you know is leading him in the wrong direction, don't just stand there, pull him aside and talk to him. He told us that the temptations in life can sometimes be overwhelming, so we all need to support one another. This, he said, is what makes a clan strong. They are always united, and they always act as one, just like that chain. He told me that whenever I start to feel down, I should stop and ask myself whether I feel like the weak or the strong link.

Over the years I have had the opportunity to meet and work with many different Elders and spiritual advisors from all over Indian Country. These people have shared one particular and constant teaching with me: pray for your enemies. Doing this only makes you that much stronger. Anyone who has bad feelings toward you or says something against you is someone you should be praying for. When you do this, you not only help them, but you help yourself.

They would tell me to pity these people rather than having bad feelings toward them, because they don't realize they are only making you stronger and weakening themselves when they do these things to someone else. So, pray for them and give thanks for the teaching they are giving to you.

They told me that this was the reason I had to stop feeling so much negativity and hatred for the Catholic Church, because I was giving them my spirit and allowing them to control my emotions. Anytime someone else is in control of your happiness, you make them that much stronger, because they can see they are in control.

Whenever someone goes out of their way to make you angry, just smile and tell yourself you are in control. Then turn your smile toward these people and tell them to have a nice day. You will see that soon enough they will stop bothering you, because they can see they are unable to push your buttons.

The Elder told me that he once overheard someone at a Sundance telling a young man he needed to stop talking so badly about that Jesus fellow. They told the young man that Jesus was actually a very powerful Medicine Man. They said to look at all the sick and dying people he helped. They told the young man to consider all the sick and dying people for a minute, and then to ask himself if it sounded like the work of a bad person.

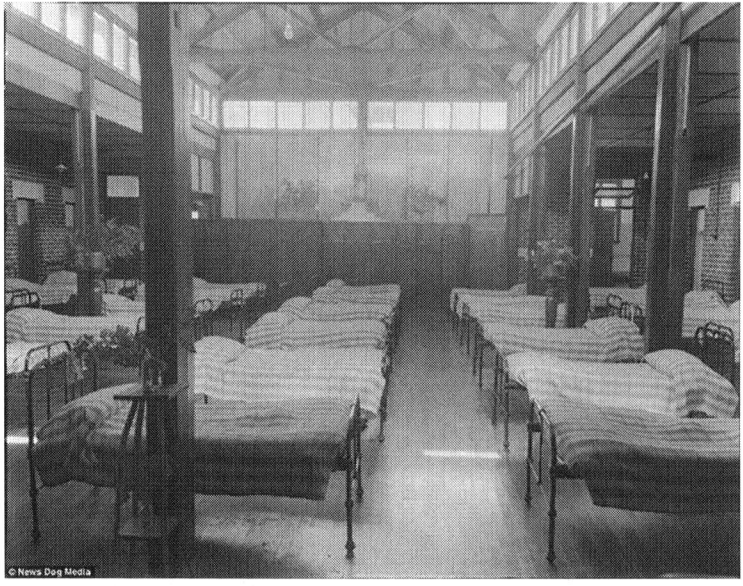

Overcrowded dormitories were one of the main causes of tuberculosis.

Chapter 4

A few years ago, I was doing some contract work for the Chehalis Indian Band near the town of Agassiz in the Fraser Valley of BC. Although I am not from this Indian Band, most of the people have gotten to know me quite well through my participation in many of the ceremonies carried out on the reserve.

My main job on the reserve was doing park maintenance and cleanup, but I also took part in a lot of community-service work in my spare time, things like cutting firewood for the local Elders or for the long house. Other times I would help with repairs to the community lacrosse rink or soccer field. As we worked, I often shared with people about my troubled childhood and being a residential school survivor. They all seemed to be sincere with the interest they showed, so I did not mind answering any of the questions they came up with.

One day I was doing some work on the grounds in front of the reserve band office when I was approached by a couple of ladies who were with the group Mothers Against Drunk Drivers. They asked me if I would consider coming to a gathering the following day and speaking to a small group of students from Agassiz High School. Without giving it much thought I said sure, I would be happy to give it a try. This was something I had never done before.

You have to remember that, like most survivors, I was timid about things like this. I try to be quiet and stay out of sight. I had never spoken openly in front of anyone I had not been given at least a couple of weeks to get to know. I usually like to spend a little time talking to people so I can get a sense of what type of person they are on the inside.

Nevertheless, I had committed myself, so I would have to at least show up in the morning and give it my best. I tried to convince myself that it could not possibly be all that bad; after all, the ladies did say that it was a just a small group of students from the local high school along with a few of their teachers. I convinced myself it was probably a dozen or so people at the most.

The next morning, after first clearing it with the Chief and then my boss—who was more than happy to give me the morning off with pay for something like this—I walked into the auditorium and felt my knees go weak. My heart felt as though it was going to jump through my chest. There I was, standing in the front door of the local auditorium with approximately two hundred students along with their teachers and a few of the local Elders all looking at me with huge smiles on their faces. It was a moment I will not forget.

I said to myself, *What the hell did I get myself into now?* It took me a few more seconds to gather myself, but as I stood there on the stage waiting to be introduced, I looked down at all the faces said a short prayer while holding tight to the small stone that one of my Elders had given me earlier that morning for strength.

He told me that all I had to do was hold it carefully in the palm of my left hand when I was speaking, and it would give me all the strength I needed to accomplish what I needed to do. He told me that if I just said a short prayer and asked the Creator for strength, he would see to it that the right words came into my heart. This, he said, was something he always did whenever he was going to do something for the first time.

As I began to speak about my experiences, not only in residential school, but on the streets and in prison, I saw the looks of interest on the faces seated before me. Although I found it difficult at first to talk about some of the more extreme abuse, I somehow managed to get myself through it.

By the time I was finished speaking it had been well over an hour and I began feeling so at ease up there that I thought I could go right on talking for the rest of the day. It was difficult to explain, but I suddenly felt as though a huge weight had been lifted off my shoulders, and I had a sense of absolute relief from opening up and letting go of everything inside. My experience that day was so good that I decided to keep that little stone and added it to my medicine pouch.

Later that day, when I finished speaking to the students and we were all sitting down to enjoy the lunch that was provided for us, one of the local Elders came over to our table and introduced herself to me. She had tears in her eyes as she thanked me for speaking, and she told me that she too was a survivor, but she was never able to speak openly about it like I had. Her words meant so much more to me than she could have possibly realized, and I went home later that day feeling proud and fulfilled.

Since that day I have never allowed myself to walk away from any opportunity to speak to people about my personal experiences, whether to a group of people or just one individual. The experience I received on that day has taught me that if I can possibly help someone else to understand a little more about what the residential school system did to the First Nations people, I should be satisfied and grateful for the opportunity to share. Ever since that day I simply refuse to be silent any longer.

Like many of the other survivors, I received money from the government for both the Common Experience Payment and the much lengthier Independent Assessment Process. Through it all I have heard many people, usually non-Natives, say we did not deserve the money that was paid out to the survivors, because when all is said and done the education, we received was still free and they had to pay for theirs.

Every time something would come up on television or in the newspapers regarding residential schools, these same people would say things like, "Come on already, get over it," or, "How much more whining are they going to do?" Sometimes I would have to walk out of the room to avoid getting angry. These people have no idea how deep the wounds are that we must carry for the rest of our lives.

At one point in my life, I would have responded to these individuals with anger and probably violence, but instead I think about what my Elders have taught me regarding people like this. So, I usually just walk away and say a prayer for them, because something must be very wrong in their lives to fill them with that much ugliness and negativity.

When I tell them to sit and think for a minute about how they would feel if the government went into their homes tomorrow, took all their children, and put them someplace where they could be abused, most of them say they would never be foolish enough to allow something like that to happen. In the end I cannot do anything except feel sorry for them, because they are too lost in their own ignorance to hear how foolish they sound. I can only continue to pray for them.

In the summer of 2012, while I was living and working in the city of Kamloops, I had the opportunity to spend the day visiting the old residential school that is still standing there along the Thompson River. I had been driving past this place every day on my way to and from work for three and a half months without acknowledging it. I knew from listening to other people that it was the old boarding school, but I never planned to stop there. As a matter of fact, I did my best not to even glance in that direction.

One day after work I had to stop at the grocery store to pick up a few things for supper. While I was standing in the checkout line to pay for my groceries, I noticed an old friend of mine I had not seen in seven years. He told me he was in town taking part in a job training program sponsored by the Kamloops Indian Band at the old residential school facility. He asked me if I would like to come to their graduation ceremony and feast the following week as his guest. Since it was in the evening, I reluctantly decided to accept the invitation.

The graduation ceremony was being held in the old school's dining hall and kitchen area. As I sat there looking around, I could not help feeling emotional, because not only was this my first time visiting one of these old school sites in over thirty-seven years, but the similarities to my old school were so uncanny it was like I was back in Saskatchewan sitting in the school at Lebret.

There were a lot of guest speakers from all over British Columbia who were invited to give a few words of encouragement to the graduating students. Some of them were Elders from the local reserves who were themselves former students of that very school. I listened closely to what they had to say. Most of the Elders said how happy it made them to finally see something good coming out of that old school building and to hear young people laughing.

Not only did these Elders have a lot of wonderful teachings to pass on to the graduates, but they were also able to offer a lot of insight into what it was like living there as a child in the Kamloops Indian School. They shared how they were able to heal and let go of the bad feelings they once carried toward the old school. This helped me immensely, because I too was able to finally begin to let go of a lot of the old demons I had been carrying around for decades.

Although I knew in my mind this was not the same school I attended as a child, it felt as though I was touring it. From the moment I walked through the entrance of the building I was easily able to point out where everything was located. It was almost as though I had been through the building before.

I showed everyone the way to the chapel, and where to find the dining hall. As we began walking down the long and narrow hallway toward the boys' playroom, I could feel the hairs on the back of my neck stand up. It was like I could feel the spirits of the people long since gone. At times I even began finding it difficult to breathe, and my legs began to feel weak. It became so bad at one point that I had to hold on to the wall as we slowly proceeded down a long, dark, and narrow passageway. I have never experienced anything like it before or since.

One of the people I was walking around with that day was himself a former student of this very school. He was now in his early seventies and told us that he returns quite often, just to say a short prayer and honour the memories of his old schoolmates, most of whom are now long gone. He said there was a time he too couldn't bring himself to look at the old site, let alone visit it.

As we talked, he told us that he still feels anxiety every time he walks into the building. He showed us to a small porch that was now being used as an emergency exit. He said that back when he attended school there it was the boys' entrance. All along the side walls there were large metal hooks that were used to hang shovels so the boys could clear snow from the sidewalks during the cold winter months, something he had done for years.

He told us that back when he was nine years old, he and a small group of boys were sent out to do that very job. When they were dressed up and ready to go, they noticed that one of their friends was not there. He had been told specifically by the supervisor to go out and help. The group of boys decided to go ahead without him and proceeded to the porch, and when they opened the door to get the shovels, they found him. He had hung himself from one of those metal hooks using a skate lace. The Elder told us that he still has nightmares about that terrible incident, even though more than sixty years has passed.

I had no difficulty in believing his sad story, because I knew that this young boy was only one of thousands who died in these schools. When I first started working on my own presentation to the Truth and Reconciliation committee, I was startled to learn that over 6,000 First Nations children had died while they were in the care of the Canadian government's residential school system. This number, I was told, comes from the government's own files.

As we continued to walk with the Elder, he told us stories that sounded all too familiar. There were all kinds of stories about abuse, both physical and sexual. Most of it came from staff, but sadly, he said, there was abuse perpetrated by other students. He told us stories about hungry children and about sometimes having to steal food to feed themselves. He took us outside and showed us where the old root cellar was located. He told us how they would steal vegetables and go down along the river to cook them using an old jam pail for a cooking pot. As he spoke, I could feel the pain in his voice, and I had to fight back tears.

He told us how some of the older boys who worked in the barns would fill their pockets with the chop that was used to feed the school's horses. These boys would use an old pail of some sort to cook the chop into a kind of porridge that they would all sit around and share. It wasn't very nutritious, but it filled their bellies and stopped the hunger pains, at least temporarily. It also helped them to warm their bellies in the cold winter months.

Our two schools may have been thousands of miles apart, his here in the middle interior of British Columbia and mine in the south-central part of Saskatchewan, but the similarities were unbelievable. Not only were the building structures almost identical, right down to the materials used to build them, but the horror stories were all the same—only the faces were different. Both schools not only had to deal with things like hunger and malnutrition, but most of us had to survive through sicknesses like chicken pox, measles, mumps, and tuberculosis, diseases that were rampant in these schools.

I remember being told we were extremely lucky because we were still alive. There were plenty of other kids who I can recall leaving for hospital and never seen again. It was not until much later in my life that I found out the sanatorium where they sent sick children was only a few miles away from the school. People referred to it as "Fort San," because it was near the town of Fort Qu'Appelle. It was just at the other end of the lake, right across from our school in Lebret. Not that it would have mattered much to a bunch of young children, because most of us were way too afraid to even consider leaving the school grounds.

Most survivors will tell you that as children we received little or no actual medical care. The only regular care that any of us got came from the school nurse, who was usually one of the Catholic nuns assigned to the nursing station. The only things she ever gave out were aspirin and bandages. Sometimes in the winter months she would have cough syrup for everyone who needed it.

My younger sister once broke her arm and they did nothing for her until a few days later, after they realized she wasn't just pretending like they thought. She had no use of her arm, and she would scream whenever someone tried to make her move it. Anyone with even the slightest medical training would have reached the conclusion that something was wrong with her arm.

Once every year a dentist was brought in to check our teeth, and an optometrist was brought in to check our eyes. Other than that, we rarely saw an actual doctor unless we were considered to have a severe enough injury to warrant the drive to the local hospital in the nearest town. When we required vaccinations, they were usually given to us by one of the community health nurses from the area, who would stop by the school and give everyone their shots at the same time.

On more than one occasion when I was suffering from some sort of ailment, I found myself confined to my bed in the main dormitory. These were the toughest of days for a small child, because we had no one there to comfort us or keep us company. If we were lucky, we were only there for the day; other times we could find ourselves confined for up to a week. This depended on what type of ailment we were suffering from and whether they thought we should be quarantined.

The dormitories were large rooms containing row after row of homemade wooden bunk beds, all painted white. There was a row of large sinks along one side of the room where we were all lined up every night to wash up and prepare for bed. Then we would grab our toothbrushes and be given some awful-tasting white powder to brush our teeth with before going to bed. If we tried to get out of it, we were immediately yelled at in front of everyone else.

When one of us was unfortunate enough to become sick, we were confined to the dormitory area and told to stay in our own bed. There was no television or radio to help pass the time, so we were often bored, unless there was more than one person sick. We did not even have books or magazines to keep our minds busy. The meals would be brought to us by one of the nuns who would also distribute any medications that were being prescribed to us.

Other than these brief visits, we saw no one for the entire day. Only at ten o'clock in the evening would all the other children appear one by one and begin the same nightly ritual all over again. Depending on how sick we were, the supervisor would make us get up and join in the routine along with everyone else.

Most of us learned not to say anything when we were feeling slightly sick or under the weather. No one wanted to end up alone in the dorm for what would often end up being days at a time, especially if it meant being stuck up there during the summer months when it was beautiful outdoors. Being typical children, we did not even like being stuck in the classroom when we could be outdoors enjoying ourselves.

Then there were the weekends when we would have to listen to the sounds of the other children running around laughing and playing games on the playground. Most of the children were afraid to become sick because we were made to feel as though we were being punished if we came down with something.

Fortunately, those of us who were considered sick enough to wind up in the dormitory were generally so sick we did not care what they did to us. Those individuals fortunate enough to have only developed a common cold or a mild fever considered themselves to be lucky, because they could still manage their daily routines without worrying about being stuck in the dorm area by themselves.

Regardless of the hardships our people have been forced to endure over the past four hundred years, we are still here, alive and stronger than ever. Despite all the attempts by the government and Church to eradicate our people by trying to destroy every trace of our cultural and our spiritual teachings, we have managed to survive. In fact, we are stronger than ever because of the greater number of our people graduating with degrees. Even most of our Native languages have managed to survive.

I used to be angered by all of this, but today I am filled with extreme pride. This is because our people found it within themselves to forgive their perpetrators and move on in life. Our people decided it was better to focus more on healing than on hating. This is thanks to the unbelievable strength of our Elders and their teachings.

This was accomplished by returning to those very teachings that everyone tried so hard to take away from us. That is why I tell the younger generation that there is strength in what the Elders are trying to teach them, they just need to take the time to listen. The sad part is that most young people think they do not need advice from anyone. And truthfully, we were all the same way when we were their age.

Remember that two of the most basic human needs are to love and be loved. Still, some people will try to convince you they can get through life all on their own, that they don't need anything from anyone. Most often this kind of behaviour comes as a result of some sort of pain they experienced somewhere in their past.

Usually, it is because trusting someone in the past has ended badly for them. Now they simply choose to trust no one.

Opening our hearts to someone only to end up being let down or disappointed never feels good and can cause people to shut down and stop communicating with the world around them. Many of us will do this by making it look as if we have it all together and we need nothing from anyone. We learned how to walk around all day with a fake smile that helps to hide our pain, and this helps to convince everyone who sees us that we are pleasant individuals.

I lived like this for years, pretending that everything was all right while refusing to open up and talk to anyone about anything. I was content just trying to drown my problems in a pitiful world of drugs and alcohol. Somehow this seemed easier than taking the time to learn how to trust anyone again and risking more disappointment. Deep down I was lonely and afraid, but I chose to pretend that everything was fine.

When I was young and just out of residential school, I was one of those people who wanted nothing from anyone, because up until that point in my life I felt everyone I came into contact with wanted something from me and didn't give a damn about what I wanted. Those very people, who were supposed to care for me and provide me with an education and someplace safe to live, were abusing everyone around them. They did not care whether what they were doing was scarring us emotionally or not.

This taught me to shut everyone out and trust solely in my own abilities to survive. Therefore, I know exactly what it means to go through life thinking that you do not need anything from anyone else. The few times I did try to reach out to people for help and protection, I was punished and called a liar for speaking out. Never again would I trust in the system to do the right thing. From now on I would be the only one in charge of my destiny.

Now that I was finally free from the evil clutches of the residential school system, I realized I had no place else to go. At first, I tried returning to the reservation and the family I vaguely remembered, but they had all changed and were not prepared to have me come walking back into their lives after eleven years. I was now an outsider with no real ties to the reserve. This meant that I was free to go anywhere I pleased—not that there were a lot of options available to me.

After some harsh words were exchanged between me and my mother's new boyfriend, I found myself on the streets of Regina with nothing but the clothes on my back. There I was, just short of my sixteenth birthday, fresh out of school, and forced to learn how to fend for myself on the city streets. Still, I told myself at least I was my own boss, and I did not have to answer to anyone. As far as I was concerned, I was probably better off without them anyway.

It may have seemed difficult at first, but like everything else in my young life I learned how to adapt quickly and survive on my own. I even convinced myself that after surviving the past eleven years in those awful residential schools, I could pretty much handle anything that the world could throw at me. I told myself that nothing had really changed, aside from my location. The world was still filled with predators, and I had to learn to be careful of whom I allowed myself to trust or associate with. It was me against the world from that day forward.

After a few days of fending for myself I joined up with a group of other young Native kids who were all in the same boat as me: being homeless with no family to turn to for assistance or guidance. Together we quickly learned how to survive and provide for ourselves one day at a time. We went from living in back lanes, sleeping in old cars and abandoned buildings, to cheap motel rooms we rented by the week or by the month, depending on how successful our week was. All I can say is that we never went hungry.

Together we had our own ways of hustling and coming up with our share of the money we needed to pay rent and feed ourselves. Sometimes, when the panhandling did not work, we took to rolling drunks as they left the bars at closing time. Most times this resulted in us going home for the night with alcohol and cigarettes, as well as money. This aided in our now increasing use of drugs and alcohol, which was getting worse by the day.

We knew where to go if we needed clean clothes or a quick meal. Most times when we needed something we took it from wherever we could get it, without worrying about who we hurt in the process. Sometimes we would sit around our motel room at night and laugh about how close we came to getting caught.

We knew that what we were doing was wrong, even illegal, but we didn't care. We had been victimized for so long that we looked at what we were doing as getting even or taking back what we had lost. I can remember hearing my friends' saying things like, "Don't worry about it, they owe us a lot more than this."

When we did get caught and ended up spending a few months in the provincial correctional centre, we laughed about it. We would tell each other that this was no different than being in residential school all over again. They even gave us another institutional number to identify ourselves by, just like back in school. This place was not anything new to us; we were used to having our lives dictated to us by people working for the government.

From the time we got up in the morning until we went to bed at night there was someone around to tell us what to do. We were told when to eat and when we could go outside for exercise. We were told what to wear and when we could wear it. When I talked with other survivors who were in jail with us, they said that jail was easy because we were institutionalized long before we got there. This was a statement I could not argue with.

Prison is the modern-day version of the old residential school system, and that is why all these institutions are so full of Indigenous men and women. Although the First Nations people make up only approximately 4 percent of the population in Canada, we make up 24 percent of the people who are incarcerated. Someone said that there are nearly as many First Nations people in jail as there are living on the reserves. This made me open my eyes.

At first, I thought this sounded farfetched, but considering the number of prisons in this country I'm forced to give this statement some serious consideration. Besides, all the jails I was unfortunate enough to find myself in were nearly all filled with Natives. Some places were at least 80 percent First Nations. I cannot remember being in a correctional facility that had less than 50 percent of our people making up the population. This includes both federal and provincial facilities.

An awful lot of people, including some who come from our very own First Nations communities, will say that we as survivors should not be using all our negative experiences as an excuse for the way our lives have turned out. Most of the time these are individuals who have never experienced the residential school system themselves, yet they will speak about the subject as though they are authorities on it. They refuse to believe that any of those terrible experiences that many of us suffered through as children could possibly have any kind of negative effect on our adult lives.

Most of these people will go on to tell me that they know a lot of different people who have attended residential school at some point in their lives. They will explain to me that these people have all lived perfectly normal lives without becoming alcoholic, ending up in jail, or living on the street. Some of these people have gone on to become the chief of their community. Others have become successful business owners. Then they try to convince me that many of these survivors have much better lives then they do.

All I can say to this is that I do not doubt them or what they are saying, because I also know that not everyone was victimized the same way in all the schools. We did not all share the same experiences any more than the rest of the world did. I believe that the perpetrators only picked on children who were younger and more vulnerable. Those who couldn't fight back. I say this because

I know from experience that the older, I got, the less they paid attention to me.

I refuse to let what any of these people say anger me, because these are usually the very people who tell you the reason their children are all running around in gangs and not only selling but using drugs is because of white society in general. They will continuously blame racism and the fact they are stuck on the reserve for their kids' problems and behaviours.

I can't help feeling sorry for their children, because it is usually Native against Native in these gang fights. It seems to me that if they are so angry at the non-Native world, why are they so busy fighting each other? Surely there are other ways of protesting the system that does not require joining a street gang and fighting your own people.

Maybe if these parents took time to teach their children a little about their own culture and spirituality, they would finally have something to be proud of, rather than running around feeling angry all the time. It is amazing just how much strength people get from learning about their own culture and spirituality. This is something I try to emphasize whenever I am given the opportunity talk to the youth in various communities.

When I first joined that Healing Circle some thirty years ago, I remember the Elder asking the participants to raise their hands if they thought the white man was responsible for their problems. As you can imagine, practically everyone in the room had their hands up. The Elder promptly informed us that we were all wrong, because we had one thing in life that the Creator gave to each one of us: choice. That is the one thing no one can take away from you. Whether we make the right choice is something that falls upon each of us.

He told us that no one twisted our arms when we went out and got drunk or did any of the other stupid things that we were responsible for throughout our lifetimes. He pointed out that every one of us in that circle was responsible for his own choices in life.

He told everyone that they needed to learn to man up and accept that as fact if we ever wanted to make positive changes in our lives. Once we have done this, we will become positive examples for the younger people in our community.

Our Elder told us to consider John Trudell from a well-known activist group, the American Indian Movement, who said that our battle is not with the white man, it is with their government. He reminded everyone that it is the government that implements all the policies and laws that hurt and hold back the people. It is them we need to change if we are going to create change in the people or the country.

That same Elder went on to point out that every young man likes to think of himself as a warrior, but when you ask him what that means, he hasn't got the slightest clue. He told us that most young people today have a mixed-up view of how things are supposed to be. Most of them have an idea that being a warrior means running around attacking everyone for no reason. They don't know that a true warrior places everyone else before himself and takes care of everyone else's needs before considering his own. A true warrior is first a provider for his community and then he is a protector. Not for himself, but for the people.

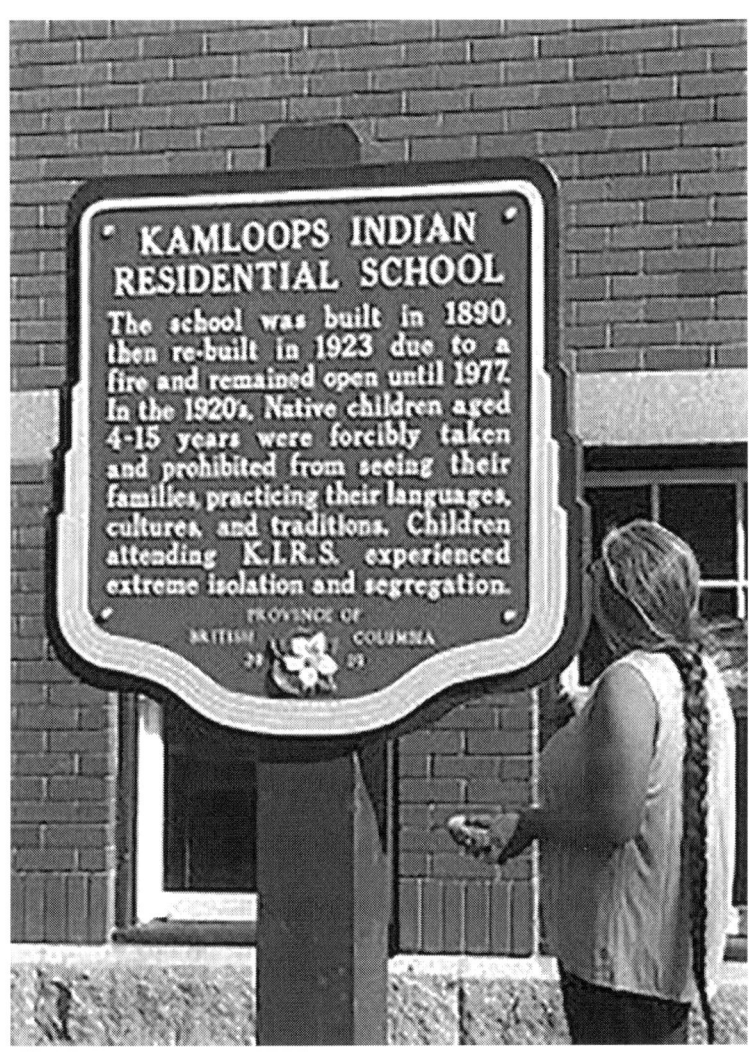

Chapter 5

It is true that everyone has the right to believe whatever they choose in life. However, even the Supreme Court of Canada has stated that a person's childhood experiences, and personal upbringing can, and does, affect their adult life. They made all this clear when they rendered their decision in connection to the court case that has become known simply as the "Gladue Decision."

The Supreme Court of Canada has directed all the lower courts that when it comes to the sentencing of First Nations offenders, they must first consider all other avenues available before considering incarceration. The National Parole Board of Canada was directed to apply all its decision-making in accordance with their ruling whenever they deal with decisions regarding the release of any First Nations offender. This ruling carries with it a strong message surrounding the treatment and abuse of First Nations people.

The Gladue Decision tells the lower courts that when they are dealing with First Nations people, they must take into consideration the childhood and upbringing of the defendant when it comes to sentencing or granting them parole. They must take into consideration whether the defendant was a residential school survivor, whether they lived on a reservation, whether they lived in poverty, whether they grew up in an alcoholic setting and whether they were abused as a child or exposed to family violence of any sort. This ruling clearly tells the world that all these negative things can and do affect an individual's adult life.

Today when I hear any of our spiritual leaders speaking about the Seven Sacred Teachings, I fill with pride in who I am, but part of me will always be sad, because I could not teach any of these things to my own children and grandchildren. These were lost to us in the residential schools. If we tried to talk about things like this we were severely punished and told these were not the lord's teachings, because they did not come from his Holy Bible.

These Seven Sacred Teachings are love, respect, bravery, honesty, humility, truth, and wisdom. These, I thought, were all the same teachings they claimed came from their own Holy Bible, yet somehow our versions were wrong. When I tried to ask one of the nuns about this, she gasped at me and said this was blasphemy. She told me that I should beg God for his forgiveness for allowing myself to think such things. Eventually I gave up trying to understand. I thought the teachings just confused everyone and made life difficult anyway.

A few years ago, I had a long, drawn-out discussion with a minister from one of the local community churches. As we talked, I deliberately pointed out that the entire Church and its religion is based upon stories or legends, depending on how you choose to look at it. I told him that as a child I was forced to listen to, as well as read, a lot of these Bible stories.

I told him the majority of our teachings from the Elders are in the form of stories as well, so I didn't see a difference. We also have our own creation stories, as well as stories about evil beings and healers. The only difference is that we don't have anyone named "Jesus." I pointed out to him that one of the Church's greatest stories has to do with the coming of Jesus and how he was seen as the saviour of the people. Likewise, our most well-known stories cover the coming of a sacred lady referred to simply as "White Buffalo Calf Woman," and how she first brought the Sacred Pipe to the First Nations people. This pipe was meant to heal and unite the people. Today, whenever people talk about that original pipe, they still refer to it as the "White Buffalo Calf Pipe."

When I later asked this minister how they could possibly believe in their own heaven or in saints and angels while condemning the First Nations people for believing in spirits, spirit helpers, or in the Spirit World, he replied that he had no answers for me, but he thought my question was a fair one. I could tell my questions were making him uncomfortable.

I told him I found it to be ironic that their angels and our spirit helpers sounded so much alike. The same could be said regarding their heaven and our Spirit World. I often wondered if there was a difference between the two. In the end he just laughed and said that sometimes people just refuse to accept anything they don't understand or have complete control over. People fear anything that is different, and rather than sit down and try to talk about things, they will condemn it and try to turn everyone away from it. This, unfortunately, is just the way life is.

The story of the Sacred Pipe is one I remember hearing as far back as I can recall. Although there have always been a great many variations of the story, the one that I have always preferred comes from the Sioux Nation. I have always preferred this version of the story because this pipe still exists to this day, while people from other nations can never really give any kind of explanation when asked as to the whereabouts of their first pipe.

This has always been one of my favourite stories of all time, because it explains how the Sacred Pipe has been cared for and passed on from generation to generation for hundreds of years. In my own lifetime there have been three different people who held this responsibility.

In 1966, the sacred White Buffalo Calf Pipe bundle was in the care of a woman named Lucy Bad Warrior, who had received it from her brother, Eli Bad Warrior. Lucy was told in a dream to pass the sacred pipe on to her grandson, Arvol Looking Horse, who was only twelve at the time. Arvol then became the nineteenth-generation keeper of the original Sacred Pipe. He is still the current keeper of the Sacred Pipe bundle, and lives near a place called Green Grass on the Cheyenne River Sioux reservation. When the time comes, he too shall pass the bundle on to his chosen successor. In fact, some people have said that he is already teaching the young boy who will one day take his place as the twentieth generation to become keeper of the sacred White Buffalo Calf Pipe bundle, which I have come to know as the "People's bundle."

Whenever the Elders would speak to us about this, I would listen intently and take in their every word with excitement and wonder. I can recall how the Elders would describe the Sacred Pipe as though they had just handled it moments ago, carefully describing it with reverence and respect.

They would describe the four ribbons hanging from the stem and explain how they represented the four quarters of the universe. The black one is for the west, where the Thunder Beings live to send us the rain; the white one is for the north, which sends us the great white cleansing wind; the red one is for the east, which sends us the light and is where the morning star lives to give men wisdom; the yellow is for the south, which gives us summer and the power to grow things. But these four spirits, they would say, are only one spirit after all, and the eagle feather hanging alongside the four ribbons is for that one, which is like a father, and it is for the thoughts of men, which should rise as high as the eagles.

The Lakota version of the coming of the Sacred Pipe has been told to children for hundreds of years. I know it so well I can almost repeat it word for word. This is how I remember hearing it: A very long time ago, they say, two scouts were out looking for buffalo. When they came to the top of a high hill and looked north, they saw something coming a long way off in the distance. Finally, when it came closer, they both cried out, "It is a woman!" and it was. And then one of the scouts, being foolish, had bad thoughts about the beautiful woman and spoke them, but the other one said, "This is a sacred woman. Throw all bad thoughts away." When she came still closer, they saw that she wore a fine white buckskin dress, her hair was very long, and she was young and very beautiful. And she knew their thoughts and said in a voice that was like singing, "You do not know me, but if you want to do as you think, you may come." And of course, the foolish one went, but just as he stood before her there was a white cloud that came and covered them both. The beautiful young woman came walking out of the cloud, and when it blew away the foolish man was nothing, but a skeleton covered with worms.

The young woman spoke to the warrior who was not foolish, "You should go and tell your people that I am coming and that a big tepee shall be built for me in the centre of the nation." And the young man, who was now very much afraid, went quickly and told the people, who did at once as they were told, and there around the big tepee they waited for the sacred woman. And before long she came, very beautiful and singing, and as she went into the tepee, this is what she sang:

> *With visible breath I am walking*
> *A voice I am sending as I walk*
> *In a sacred manner I am walking*
> *With visible tracks I am walking*
> *In a sacred manner I walk.*

And as she sang, there came from her mouth a white cloud that was good to smell. Then she gave something to the Chief, a pipe with a bison calf carved on one side to mean the earth that bears and feeds us, with twelve eagle feathers hanging from the stem to mean the twelve moons, and these were tied with a grass that never breaks. "Behold!" she said. "With this you shall multiply and become a good, strong nation. Nothing but good shall ever come from it. Only the hands of the good shall take care of it and the bad shall not even see it." She began singing again and went out of the tepee, and as the people watched her going, suddenly she was a white buffalo galloping away and snorting, and soon she was gone, off into the distance again.

The song that she sang in the story may not have any meaning to non-Native people, but it is a powerful song that can still be heard today whenever the original pipe of the people is brought out in the different ceremonies. Those who follow the sacred ways and know some of the teachings that come with the Sacred Pipe also know the meaning, as well as the significance of the song she sang.

To the First Nations people the Sacred Pipe carries the same sacredness as the Bible or the sacraments. When we take a sacred oath or make a commitment, we hold the pipe as we recite our vow; when white men take an oath, they hold the Bible. To our people the Sacred Pipe is one of the most sacred objects that we as a people have. It is the one thing that we all recognize as being truly sacred.

Only when we all learn how to accept this, and respect each other's ways, can we successfully begin to work together for the improvement of the world in which we are all forced to live side by side. Every nation requires the same genuine respect and acceptance in order to thrive and advance in a healthy and sacred manner. This is the Creator's wish for all of mankind.

The Elders tell us there cannot be anything wrong with any religion or spiritual practice if it helps even one person. We must begin by learning not to condemn something just because we do not understand it; we should always listen with an open heart, taking only what we need from the teaching and leave the rest.

If we see or hear things we do not agree with, we leave those things behind. We are only obligated to practice the things we truly believe in. No one can tell us how to pray or who to pray with. This is our birthright as First Nations people and it is protected under the UN's Universal Declaration of Human Rights.

Marieval Indian residential School on the Cowessess First Nation in Southern Saskatchewan. This is where 750 unmarked graves are located, adding to the growing number.

Chapter 6

In 1990, when I was initiated into the Dakota Wolf Clan by my Elder and spiritual teacher, I decided to make a commitment to follow the sacred teachings of the pipe and sweat lodge. The first two things I was required to do were offer both cloth and tobacco to my Elder, then ask if he would be my teacher. Before accepting any of my offerings, he folded his arms and asked if this was something I was absolutely sure I wanted to do.

He told me if I went through with this, I had to be ready to give him the next seven years of my life, because that is how long it was going to take me to complete this commitment. When I said yes, he took the offerings and told me, with a huge smile on his face, that I now belonged to him for the next seven years. I knew that it wasn't going to be easy, but I wanted to make changes in my life and to feel that I was doing something worthwhile after all the years of wasting my life following the Black Road.

Within the next few weeks, I learned exactly why he had that huge smile on his face when he was accepting my offering. As we sat silently around the fire preparing for our weekly sweat lodge ceremony, he told me there were going to be times when I would get frustrated and even angry with him. He said I might even begin to hate him and want to walk away from everything that he was trying to teach me. Most people do, he said, but they usually come back once they have had enough time to cool down and refocus their thoughts.

This lifestyle, he told me, is far from easy, and people sometimes become overwhelmed, especially if they feel that everything is happening too fast. He told me that people sometimes think he is being too strict, but he is just trying to teach them about discipline. He reminded me that everything he was going to teach me would come in handy soon, so I had better get used to it.

We must remind ourselves that walking on the Red Road is much harder, because it requires us to change and give up all of our old negative lifestyle, including friends as well as habits. No matter how we look at it, being good is always harder than being bad.

He was right about how I was going to become frustrated and angry from time to time, and how I was going to want to walk away and call it quits. Whenever this would happen, he would say, let's talk, and I will remind you of why you are here in the first place. He would tell me to remember the teachings I have been given over the years and to use them. After all, I was the one who chose this lifestyle. No one was forcing me to be there.

He talked about how the Creator never gives us more than we can handle. He reminded me that nothing happens in life without a reason. He would tell me to pray when I become frustrated. This, he told me, would stop me from becoming angry and doing or saying something that I don't really mean. In the end he always knew just what to say to calm me down.

The first few years working with him were extremely busy and often exhausting. Sometimes there were as many as four or five sweat lodge ceremonies in one week, and I was expected to attend each one. Sometimes I was told to go inside and help with the praying, other times I was told to act as a helper outside, preparing the fire and readying the lodge. I also had to learn how to fill and care for the pipe in accordance with the teaching of my Elder and his teachers before him. I took this responsibility very seriously.

Then there were all the songs we were required to sing. Each round in the lodge required two or three different songs in certain succession. There were different songs for filling the pipe, prayer songs, tobacco-offering songs, calling songs, four-direction songs, thank-you songs, honour songs, and songs for practically every other occasion that you can think of.

I also had to learn how to make prayer ties and flags to hang in the lodge whenever I was present for the ceremony. There were certain things I was required to do each year for my Spirit Helper, and for the Indian name that was given to me when I started out on this journey. I was told these things were very important and could not be overlooked. I was told that when it comes to spirituality, I could never be lazy, because the ancestors are always watching and listening to us. They are even present when we are asleep. That, he told me, was why it was important to always think before acting or saying anything.

Some of my new clan brothers told me that at first it was difficult for them to remember all the songs and teachings too, but with patience and a lot of prayer everything comes together. They told me to keep on trying and to never give up on myself. They told me that when someone starts to doubt themselves, they usually end up running into difficulty. I took all their advice to heart, and in the end, everything became easier, and before I knew it my seven-year commitment had come and gone.

At first, I foolishly allowed myself to think, *Great! I am finally done, and things will get a whole lot easier now.* Then my clan brothers told me that it was only the easy part that was over. They laughingly told me it was like completing my apprenticeship training, and now I would have to buckle down and do the real work.

Completing the seven-year commitment only meant that I no longer required the Elder's constant supervision. I was now expected to prepare things on my own and have them ready when the Elder showed up for the ceremony. I thought the first seven years were hard, but I was about to find out that the hard part was about to begin. The first seven years was only meant to allow the Elder to see the level of commitment in the people he was teaching. By the time the first seven years was complete he would be able to tell if someone was going to be ready for the responsibility of the pipe and Sundance ceremonies.

Only now have I finally begun to fully understand what the Elder meant when he said that everything, he was teaching us was preparing us for the future. I had no sooner completed my seven-year commitment than I was told to begin preparing myself for the first of four Vision Quest ceremonies I had to complete in preparation for the Sundance. This was another sacred ceremony I was required to complete at least four times in my life.

He told me that I would be doing at least one Vision Quest ceremony a year for the next four years. If I chose to do more than one a year, I could be done that much quicker. This meant taking part in fasts, which under normal circumstances could last for as long as four days and four nights. He told me that once I had completed the four Vision Quests, I could begin preparing for the Sundance, which I was also expected to complete four times. Then I would be done.

The second year that I completed my Vision Quest, I was presented with my very own pipe to care for and use whenever I prayed. When it was first given to me, I felt so proud of myself for everything I had accomplished up to that point. Then I remembered being told a few years back that there was a lot of responsibility that came with caring for that pipe, and I felt scared.

I began questioning whether I was fully prepared for this kind of responsibility. One of my Elders told me I was expected to bring out everything that was in my bundle and smudge it regularly. This was to ensure that it was always clean, because there was no other way of ensuring that the bundle did not pick up anything negative along the way. This was all part of the responsibility.

I was told by the Elders that my life no longer belonged to me, that it now belonged to the people, and that the pipe I was carrying belonged to them and it was my responsibility to care for it like it was a part of me. One Elder told me to treat it like it was a small child, to always protect it and keep it close to me, even when I was sleeping. From that day forward I kept the pipe bundle close enough to pick up in a moment's notice.

The Elders told me that a lot of people will mistakenly pick up the pipe for the wrong reasons. Sometimes they will foolishly think there is some kind of prestige in being able to say to everyone, "I am a pipe carrier." These people don't realize that by picking up that pipe they must now place themselves last. Everyone else comes before you, because you are now a servant of the people. This is why we are told that the pipes we carry belong to the people.

The Elders told me this was a very hard life, because there will always be people and things trying to tempt me and stop me from doing what I must do. You must never touch illegal drugs or alcohol, because these things will render you useless to your people. If you do touch these things, you are not allowed to handle any sacred object, including the pipe, for four days, and you will not be able to help anyone, because the spirits will not recognize you until you are clean once again. Sometimes this requires a cleansing ceremony.

I was told that the pipe must always come first in my life, even before my loved ones. For example, I was told to imagine that my favourite little sister was getting married in July of the following year, and she told me that she really wanted me to be there for her on her big day. Then, just before the wedding, I received a call from one of my Elders asking me to bring my pipe to a Sundance on that same weekend. Where was I going to go? I had to ask myself exactly where your commitment lay.

The Elders told me that it is my duty to always follow the pipe wherever it chooses to take me, which means I had to find the strength to tell my little sister how sorry I was, but I had to go down to the Sundance, because the people needed me, and I could not let them down. This, he said, is the life that I have chosen for myself, and now I must follow it and live by the laws of the Sacred Pipe.

They told me repeatedly that I cannot put any of my personal feelings first. Even if my worst enemy comes to me for help, I am obligated to help him, no matter what he has done to me or to any of my loved ones. When it comes to situations like this, I was told it is my duty to look past my personal feelings and do what is expected of me as a pipe carrier. This is what it means to be a true servant of the people.

I was told that anytime someone comes to me offering cloth and tobacco in a sincere manner, I cannot turn them away. This is why they say being a pipe carrier is by no means an easy life to follow. The Elders will also tell you that it takes a strong person to be married to a pipe carrier, because the pipe must always take precedence over everything else in your life, even your wife and children.

Sometimes people can't understand something like this or even consider putting up with it and they will leave the relationship. It is almost like they become jealous of the Sacred Pipe and the commitment you have made to it. This is why the Elders will tell you to think long and hard before you make a commitment to living this way of life. They say that you must know exactly what you are getting yourself into or you will find yourself living a life of total disappointment.

My Elder told me that his own first marriage fell apart because of his commitment to the pipe and this way of life. He told me that regardless of how much it hurt him, he had to let her go and allow her to live her own life. When his pain eventually went away, he understood that the relationship just wasn't meant to be. He prayed about it before finally placing everything in the Creator's hands and carrying on with his life. He told me that he eventually met someone new who turned out to be his perfect partner in life.

This all meant that I had to begin learning as much about the Sacred Pipe as I possibly could. I learned that the pipes of the plains people express in the sincerest manner all that is most sacred to our people. These pipes not only have sacred origins that are often defined in rich mythologies, but there are also pervasive beliefs, held to this very day, that if ever these pipes are no longer used or respected, the people will lose their centre and cease to be a people. That is how much power our people give the pipes.

I cannot even begin to express the importance of the Sacred Pipes to our First Nations people from one end of this country to the other. Each one of these pipes is the glue that holds our Nations together, helping to keep us strong and on the right path. We use these pipes when we are praying for something, and when we are giving thanks for things we receive from our Creator. Elders will often conduct pipe ceremonies while sitting in a circle with numerous other people. However, some will use the pipe by themselves when they feel that they need to meditate or pray for something personal.

When the pipe is being filled with the sacred tobacco, prayers are offered for the powers of the universe and the numerous forms of creation, each represented by a single grain of tobacco. The smoke that rises toward the heavens is visible prayer, at the sight and fragrance of which the entirety of creation rejoices. The mysteries of the Sacred Pipe are so profound that the rite of smoking for First Nations people can be compared to the rite of Holy Communion for Christians. It is therefore not without reason that it is commonly referred to by most non-Aboriginal people as the "Peace Pipe," and was always used in establishing a relationship, or peace, between friends as well as enemies or nations.

I loved learning about these spiritual ways of our people and began taking great interest in whatever the Elders were willing to share with me. Before long I found myself being asked to act as helper to the Elder at ceremonies and gatherings. This allowed me to learn about the sweat lodge as well as the Sacred Pipe. I was told by one Elder that seven sacred ceremonies were given to us, and these were the two most used by all First Nations people on Turtle Island.

Without these first two ceremonies, we would not be able to carry out any of the other important rites, such as the Sundance or Vision Quest ceremonies. The sweat lodge—or Inipi ceremony, as the Sioux People call it—is carried out in preparation for all other major rites and are participated in prior to any kind of important undertaking. They are sacred rites of renewal, or spiritual rebirth, in which each of the four sacred elements—earth, air, fire, water—contribute to the people's physical and psychical purification.

A small dome-shaped lodge is first constructed from bent willow saplings, over which are placed buffalo hides or canvas tarps; these make the little lodge tight and dark inside. Within the lodge at its centre is a small circular pit containing rocks that have already been heated outside the lodge in a fire pit that is usually facing east. When the person who is running the ceremony begins to pour water over these hot rocks, they give off steam so that the lodge soon becomes intensely hot, and fragrant from the herbs and medicines that are sprinkled over the rocks. Specific medicines are applied to different rounds of the ceremony. I was taught that each of the materials used in the building of the lodge has its own symbolic value, as does every detail of the design and ritual usage.

The lodge itself represents the Universe, with the pit at the centre as the naval in which dwells the Great Spirit with his power, which is fire. The willows that form the frame of the lodge represent all that grows from Mother Earth. The rocks represent the earth, and the indestructible and everlasting nature of Wakan-Tanka, the Great Spirit. The water, too, reflects values for the people to learn from, because everyone knows that water is life itself. Without water there is no life. This is why Elders become upset when they see younger people playing with water, particularly during the summer Sundance season.

One year, during my early learning, some of my clan brothers were squirting each other with the hose and carrying on with idle horseplay while I prepared the lodge for our weekly ceremony. The Elder did not say anything as he sat working on his prayer ties for the ceremony, but I could see him watching them from time to time. Just before we were to go into the lodge, he told me, "You are going to be my doorman tonight."

I started to protest, saying that I had been really looking forward to that night's ceremony. The Elder smiled and said, "Trust me, you are my doorman. Just for tonight." I reluctantly obeyed and, as the ceremony began, I heard him say loudly, "So you want to monkey around with water, huh?" Then I heard a loud splash as he dumped an entire pail of water onto the rocks at one time. This was immediately followed by the sudden gasping and moaning of my clan brothers as the heat quickly filled the lodge.

The Elder explained how disappointed he was with their behaviour earlier that day. He pointed out to everyone that our relatives were out there dancing from sunup till sundown, without food or water, sacrificing themselves for us, so we should try to show a little more respect. My brothers never again played around with water after that day.

When the sweat lodge ceremony was over and everyone was quietly getting dressed, it dawned on me just how lucky I really was. When I was in residential school, I had no one to provide me with any of these teachings. Typically, I would have been slowly given these teachings by my grandparents or other community Elders as I was growing up and becoming a young adult.

They would have made sure that as I slowly grew from a child into a young man, and they felt confident enough in me to say that the time was right, I would have been given the necessary teachings to be able to participate fully in all the ceremonies commonly practiced by our people. I wouldn't have had to learn by trial and error. Like my grandparents before me, I would have completed most of these ceremonies by the time I was out of my teenage years.

I still would have had to go through the same steps I ended up going through in the long run; however, I would have been much more prepared, because I would have had someone there teaching me throughout my entire life journey, rather than having to learn everything as I participated in the event. Like Arvol Looking Horse who started caring for the sacred White Buffalo Calf Pipe bundle when he was only twelve years old, I too would have started learning when I was still considered just a young boy.

When we grow up in our own home communities, our grandparents teach us about these things from an early age. They would patiently point out each step and explain why things are done in such a manner. By the time we are old enough to begin participating in these ceremonies, we know what is expected of us because it has been lovingly instilled in us over the years.

Whenever I get the opportunity to speak to any of our youth, I try to make it one of my main points to emphasise the importance of learning and participating in cultural and spiritual events. Sure, it is always nice to attend Pow-wows and spend time visiting with our old friends and relatives from faraway places; however, the amount of positive energy and strength you get from attending the more spiritual gatherings is priceless, and something you will carry for the rest of your life.

It is difficult for me to explain the feelings you have inside, feelings that can last for days after the ceremony. You always walk away with a feeling of pride in who you are and where you come from, as well as being filled with a sense of having been cleansed both spiritually and mentally. I find that I always sleep better for days after returning from a ceremony. It feels as though I am suddenly at peace with everything around me. You can't get these feelings from anywhere else that I know of, you must experience it for yourself to understand what I am talking about.

I take a lot of pride in explaining to people about the First Nations people's idea of Holistic Healing. This approach takes into account all four areas in a person's life. They believe that you cannot heal one area without healing the others as well. These include the physical, spiritual, mental, and emotional. The idea of Holistic Healing is based upon the First Nations Medicine Wheel, which contain teachings that have been around since time immemorial. These are the teachings that define who we are as human beings.

An Elder once explained Holistic Healing to me like this: you can put a bandage and medicine on a physical wound, but that does not help you deal with what caused the wound. This might require you to do some work on healing the person's mental and emotional sides. This is why our Elders say that you cannot heal a person's life unless you are prepared to heal all four areas. If you do not fix all four at once, you are only providing them with a temporary fix. Sometimes these fixes last a month, other times you are lucky if they last a few days. Then you find the person right back where they were when you started working on them.

This process of Holistic Healing was very important when dealing with my own residential school trauma. I not only had to learn how to look after myself physically by getting away from the old and much too familiar lifestyle of substance abuse, but I also had to deal with the lack of exercise and poor diet that can often be associated with that kind of negative lifestyle. Without working on all four areas of my life, there would have been no change to my own Medicine Wheel.

If it weren't for the teachings that came with Holistic Healing, I would not have known there was any connection between the bad habits I carried and my substance abuse problems. I would never have guessed that simply changing my diet and exercising would be beneficial to my personal recovery, something I am glad to say is well on its way.

After I was able to successfully complete a couple months of sobriety, I was confident enough to begin working closely with the Elders to improve my spiritual connection with the Creator. This also improved my mental and emotional sides by allowing me to finally open and talk freely about the things I kept hidden away for so many years, things that had been preventing my forward progress.

If I hadn't discovered all of this when I did, I would never have had the ability or the confidence in myself to consider preparing for something as intense as talking formally to the members of the Canadian Senate regarding the treatment of First Nations people serving time in the Canadian correctional system. I fought for proper access to cultural and spiritual activities, as well as access to more First Nations Elders and their ceremonies.

Those of us who have followed any of the valuable work that was done by the members of the Truth and Reconciliation Commission as they travelled across the country listening to the stories from thousands of survivors can only hope it was not done in vain. We are all grateful that the government of Canada has finally acknowledged the wrongdoing done to our people for generations, offences that went unimpeded for hundreds of years. Now we must allow the healing to begin.

However, we are still waiting for them to totally acknowledge the children who died in these schools and are still unaccounted for. These numbers, according to their own records, are over 20,000 and come from every residential school in North America. The whereabouts of these missing children is something that must be answered before reconciliation can be fully accomplished. Some of these families want to know where their relatives are buried so their remains can be returned to their proper homes.

The mortality rate in some of these schools was as high as 60 percent. The Port Alberni Indian School on Vancouver Island was one of this country's most notorious schools. It was known for experiments that were carried out on First Nations children using starvation as a tool. The results of these tests were documented in the government's own medical archives, as well as in the painful testimonies of the school's survivors. This cannot be forgotten.

There were several young people from my own community who passed away while attending the school that was on our reserve. This is why I know there have been deaths within these schools. One young boy from my home community was killed by the supervisor's horse at Marieval.

One young boy from the school in Lebret was screaming and crying in the dormitory while the supervisor yelled at him to get downstairs to the playroom and sit there. He told the young boy that he would deal with him later. When the young boy, who was somewhere around eight or nine, was not quick enough, the supervisor kicked him from behind and sent him flying headfirst down the stairs. He landed on his shoulders before rolling onto his back with his mouth wide open, gasping for breath. He was trying hard to speak but he was not making distinguishable sounds, just loud choking and gurgling noises.

At first, I did not know what to make of all this, because I had never seen anyone hurt like this before. The supervisor turned his attention to the rest of us, still getting dressed, and yelled at us to hurry up and get downstairs to the playroom immediately. We all ran down the stairs past the young boy to avoid becoming the supervisor's next victim.

When we were all in the dining hall having our breakfast, we saw the young boy being put into one of the school vans and taken away. We could all see what was happening because we were lined up waiting to receive our food tray. We later overheard the supervisor telling the school principal and the priest that the young boy tripped and fell while he was running away from him. We knew this was far from the truth.

This young boy was never seen again, and when we asked about him, we were told to be quiet, and that it did not concern any of us. One of our teachers told us he was taken to the hospital in Regina and would be going straight home after that. This told us his injuries were serious. I have often wondered about this young boy and whether he survived that awful morning.

Most of us knew better than to say anything about what we saw that day, because we did not want to be the next victim of one of these so-called accidents. Besides, who exactly were we going to tell anyway? No one believed us when we tried to tell them about something we thought was wrong. We did not want to be accused of trying to cause trouble for another one of their "good Christian men."

From time to time the supervisor would catch us all looking at him and I am pretty sure he knew exactly what we were thinking. He never said a word to us about the incident, but he knew we were aware of what he had done. He stopped yelling at us after that incident and did not come back the following year after the summer holidays.

There were certain teachers who were mean to their students, like Mr. John Hickey. He was at the first school I attended in Marieval. He would hit students on the top of their heads with his bare knuckles, and when they cried out, he would say, "Do you want another left hook?" Then he would wave his knuckles over their heads as though he was getting ready to strike them again. This occurred almost daily.

Students in his classes often walked around with huge knots on their heads from his knuckles, and many of them complained of severe headaches. When I went before the independent assessment board, the adjudicator told my lawyer there was hundreds of signed affidavits stating the same story and naming this same teacher as the perpetrator. According to them he was one of the most complained-about people during the investigation process regarding any of the schools in the country.

Despite all the abuse that we endured over the years, there were moments of happiness too. Maybe these did not occur as often as we would have liked, but they were there. Most of my joyful memories came when I was alone with the small group of my closest friends. We would usually find ourselves sitting on the hillside overlooking the school, enjoying each other's company for a while in a peaceful and stress-free environment.

We would often spend the entire day enjoying the warm summer sun and talking about fun memories from our childhoods back on the reserve. This was one of the only times we could speak freely about these things without fear of being condemned or punished. In the winter months when there was snow on the ground, we would spend entire days there with our sleds, going up and down the hillside trying our best to be kids for a while. These were some of the happiest times we spent in those awful schools, moments that were all too rare.

Even at this young age I was careful when it came to picking my friends and associates. These were kids who found themselves in the same situation as me, always being picked on by the older boys, or by the supervisor who would egg the older boys on. We formed a bond that was stronger than most.

We would watch out for each other and stand up together against other students bullying someone from our small group. These friendships were the closest things to family I knew as a child, so I prized them highly. To this day there are former students I still consider to be family. I would rejoice whenever I saw any of them along my travels. Most of the time this was at one of the many Pow-wows or ceremonies I found myself at.

Despite the hardships we endured in these schools, there were staff members who were extremely pleasant to be around. They would take time to stop and inquire as to how we were doing and would even be concerned when we experienced difficulty or pain. One teacher, Mrs. Toth, was given a severe scolding by a teacher named John Ross for being too nice to her students.

He told her that we would never learn anything if she continued to baby us. He said the only thing any of us understood was a firm hand or a good, strong strap. I would hear him talking as though he was a mean person, but I don't remember him putting his hands on anyone, at least not in the few years I knew him.

Despite all his complaining, Mrs. Toth never changed the way she treated any of the children and remained one of our favourite teachers. She was fondly remembered as the teacher who gave her students treats, like a stick of gum or a lollipop, whenever they completed their assignments or took the time to clean the chalkboard for her.

Even if we didn't always do as well as she would have liked, she still praised us for giving it our very best. She reminded her students that this was one of the most important things we needed to remember in life. She would tell us we needed to do our best at whatever we faced in life. As for Mr. Ross, I heard he ended up committing suicide because his wife left him during the 1973 summer holidays.

Most former survivors will undoubtedly remember Mr. Ross as the hard-nosed math and science teacher who was also heavily involved in the school's army cadet training program that ran every Thursday evening. This was another of their brilliant ideas to teach the little Indian kids about discipline and obedience. Needless to say, it was all a waste of everyone's time.

After all the time I spent marching around in circles and learning the different drills, the only thing it did for me was show me I could put up with nearly any kind of crap this world could throw at me. There was, however, some positive things that came from my participation in their army cadet training program: it taught me how to shoot straight and properly care for a rifle. This helped improve my hunting abilities later in life, so I could feed myself and my family.

Thanks to the wonderful teachings I received since leaving the Black Road and returning to our Red Road, I am now able to openly discuss all the atrocities I have witnessed over the years without becoming angry or overwhelmed. I have learned how to openly look back at everything and acknowledge that these abuses were not only awful, but the people who committed these awful acts against children were wrong. Secondly, I am now able to say that we as a society must take up the challenge to see to it that these things never occur again.

My psychologist told me I had every right to be angry at what was done to me, because I was a victim. She pointed out that if I did not feel anything negative, then she would be concerned. Feeling something only shows that I am human, that I can heal and move forward. To me it also meant that I was clean and sober, because there was a time when I felt absolutely nothing as a result of my substance abuse.

When I was first introduced to the teachings of the Red Road back in 1989, I never paid attention to the stories I heard people telling. I thought these were tall tales that people told to their children to amuse or scare them into doing what was asked of them. I had been brainwashed in this way.

Then one day I met an Elder who was well into his nineties. He told me that at one time, before any of those awful residential schools came along and changed everything, our people were more in tune with themselves and the world around them. They had what he called a "oneness with nature and the Spirit World," which gave them powers that are all but lost to us today. These powers, he said, are still there, if we take the time to learn how to reawaken them. This will take a few more generations to accomplish, but it will be well worth the wait.

He told me how some of our people once had what the white man now calls "supernatural powers." Back then, he said, it was common, but nowadays the non-Native people think this is something that only occurs in their world. When they have this ability, they give themselves all sorts of fancy names, like "psychic," "clairvoyant," "telepathic," or even "spiritual." Then they charge big money for doing it. When we had it, we were called evil and accused of witchcraft or devil worship.

He explained how most of our people at one time had some form of gift from the Creator, and they thought nothing of it. To them it was all just a part of everyday life. They believed these powers were given to them so they could help their people. These individuals were considered medicine men in their communities and were called upon whenever their gift was needed. No matter what they were called on to do, they did it with pride and humility, because this was what they were taught.

Some people could tell you of things that were yet to come and what you should do to prepare yourself. He said they received these visions while in ceremony, or sometimes in dreams. These abilities were the main reason the white man and his government feared our spiritual practices and outlawed them. Rather than taking the time to try to understand our spiritual practices and beliefs, they found it easier to call them "devil worship" or "hocus-pocus," and declare them illegal.

Luckily there were a lot of brave people out there who quietly took it upon themselves to gather as many of our sacred ceremonies as possible and hide them away underground. When they found a secret place away from the prying eyes of the public, they continued to practice and pass on the teachings. If these people had not done this, we would have lost the majority of our old ways altogether. It is because of these people that I make every effort to pass on the teachings I have been given.

We owe a great deal of thanks to those brave people who saw fit to take it upon themselves to quietly protect as many of our cultural and spiritual practices as they could. These brave people risked being sent to prison for doing what they did. Because of their brave actions we can now travel from one end of Turtle Island to the other and still find our Sundance, Shaking Tents, Pow-wows, and other ceremonies being openly carried out.

One day the Elder told me about how back when he was a young man there were no roads on the reserve, and everyone lived miles apart. He said that no one had telephones or motor vehicles back in those early days. Back then most families, if they were lucky and hardworking, owned plow horses and good strong wagons. That was their only mode of transportation at the time. In fact, if you owned a horse and wagon, you were considered well off.

Back in those days, the Elder said as he went on with his story, his mother's family lived roughly two days away by horse and wagon, somewhere down south near the US border. He explained that because of the distance they only came to visit if there was a Pow-wow or some other large ceremony happening in the community. These were the only times that made the long trip worthwhile.

One day his mother became very sick, and as she lay in her bed ailing, his father became more and more worried and did not know what to do. She smiled at them and told them not to worry, because everything was going to be all right. She instructed them to go outside and put up the extra tepee they used for traveling. She told them they would soon have visitors, so they went outside and did as she requested.

Bright and early the next morning, his father lay there quietly in his warm bed listening to the birds singing loudly as they greeted the new day in all of its glory. Before long they were interrupted by the family dogs barking loudly, announcing someone's arrival. Much to his surprise, his aunt and her husband showed up in their wagon with all the medicines his mother would need to get better. This, he explained to me, was just one example of how our people were once able to communicate with one another just by using their minds along with the power of prayer.

Then he said that if we are ever going to get back to that way of living, we need to start now. This can only occur if we return to the teachings of our ancestors and begin to practice the ceremonies given to our people by the Creator. Those abilities are still within each of us as First Nations people; we just have to learn how to awaken them again.

The Elder told me about how the old people used to stop their vehicle or wagon on the side of the road and get out so they could put tobacco down and say a prayer before beginning a journey, whether it was long or short. This was to ensure safe travels for them and their loved ones. They would do the same thing when they arrived back home again to say thank you to the ancestors for watching over them while they were away on their journey. These are some of the simple teachings that I have tried to make part of my daily life.

I enjoyed spending time with that old man, listening to his stories of growing up living off the land. Hearing him speak also helped remind me of how our ancestors passed on the teachings through stories and legends. Our people never had any kind of written history; everything they knew came from listening to the older ones who carried the knowledge within them. That is why our Elders are considered so important within the community circle. First Nations people have never placed the elderly people in nursing homes or old folks' homes like many non-Native people do. They were always considered far too valuable to let go of. Their ageless knowledge was considered irreplaceable in the community.

Sometimes I will remind the younger people that they need to learn how to show more appreciation toward these Elders before they are gone. We are continuously hearing about Elders who have passed away, and about how much they were loved and respected within their communities, but we forget to take into consideration all the knowledge they had, now lost to us. We need to start asking these Elders to teach us while they are still with us. Most of these Elders won't just start telling you things unless you approach them and make it clear you are interested in what they have to teach.

An Elder once told me that none of them have the right to force their teachings or beliefs on another person. None of us as First Nations people have the right to tell another person how they should be living their lives, even if they are doing things that are considered blatantly wrong. We can only pray for those people and ask the Creator to open their eyes in a good way so they can see the mistakes they are making before anyone is hurt, including themselves.

Our job is only to lead by example. This means we must live our lives the way we want people around us to live. When they see we are doing well and that life is good for us, they will look for whatever it is we are doing so they can have the same good fortune. This is when they will decide to look closely at what we are doing and maybe begin to live as we do. That, he said, is the way the Creator intended for it to be.

He went on to tell me how most of the young people from today's generation refer to their life partners and children as if they were pieces of personal property. Whenever they are speaking about their loved ones, they refer to them by saying, "This is my wife," or, "These are my children," which is no different than saying "my horse" or "my gun."

He told me that we need to teach the younger people how to have more respect for those they claim to love so much. He told me that back when he was a young man coming of age, he was taken aside by one of the community Elders and told he was to always respect and treat his family as though they were special gifts from the Creator, because that is exactly what they were. The Elder said they were placed in his life to grow and learn with him, and when it was time for them to move on, he must step aside and allow them to do so, even if it hurt. Remember they too were given the gift of choice.

He said that he was told to remember that his family members were separate human beings, each with his or her own thoughts and feelings. They were also entitled to their own ideas and opinions, even if they were different from his own. Just because they were currently living with him did not mean that he had the right to tell any of them how to think and feel. They had the right to make all their own mistakes, just like him.

The Elder told him he had every right to sit down and tell his family how he felt about things and to give his personal opinion on different matters, but he had to allow them to form their own conclusions. The Elder he was talking to laughed and said, "I guess being a role model is never really easy." This is something we must learn to work extra hard at every day of our lives, but it is worth it in the end.

Life does not always work out the way that we want it to. Sometimes the person you think you are in love with does not feel the same way about you. This is when you must be strong enough to step aside and allow them to pursue their own choices in life. You must be willing to accept that you cannot force anyone to love you.

Love is one of those things in life that you are going to have to work extra hard for. If you respect the people around you and treat them like they matter, they will love you and respect you in return. If they choose to leave, you must allow them to go without harsh feelings. It's like that old saying, "If you love something let it go, and if it returns it was meant to be." This is all just another part of life.

When I was done speaking with the Elder and about to leave, he told me he had something else he felt the need to share with me, so I sat back down, and he began telling me a story that he laughingly claimed to be true. I reminded myself that as a First Nations person I should be prepared to hear a story any time I was talking with an Elder. I also told myself that I was going to have to pay attention to his story if I was to catch the teaching that undoubtedly was to come with it.

The story started off when he was given the opportunity to attend an Elders' conference in Winnipeg a few years earlier. He decided to get out and see some of the city, so he walked around for a while until he began to feel tired. He decided to get on one of the local transit buses, so he could sit back and enjoy the sights without becoming overly tired.

As the bus pulled up to a stop on its way downtown, he noticed a Native couple in their early twenties about to get on. He said he could not help but notice what a lovely couple they were, that it made him proud to be First Nations. The young lady had long, beautiful dark hair and was dressed in nice clothes. The young man had his long hair in braids, and he too wore nice, traditional clothing with a beaded buckskin jacket.

The Elder said that the first thing he thought was this was a traditionally raised young couple who were proud of their heritage. Then he thought they were probably both raised by their grandparents and given good, strong, traditional teachings.

As the young couple got on, the Elder noticed that the young man held on tightly to the young lady as though he was afraid that they would become separated. When they approached the spot where he was sitting, he could see that the young man was intoxicated. Halfway down the aisle they passed a young blond-haired man who was sitting straight up in his seat, minding his own business, with a slight smile on his face. He could not see the man's eyes, because he had on a pair of dark glasses.

As the young couple approached him, the young Native man suddenly pulled the young lady as close as possible and said to the blond-haired man, "Do you like what you see?" He made no reply and continued staring straight ahead. It was almost as though he was deliberately not paying any attention to the young couple. You could tell really infuriated the young Native man.

Once again, the Native man, now getting angrier, leaned in closer and loudly repeated, "Do you like what you see?" As he said this, he pulled hard on the young lady's arm. She was clearly in some discomfort. Finally, the blond-haired man turned and said, "Excuse me?" and leaned over in their direction. The young Native man said in an angry voice, "What's the matter with you, are you blind or something?" The blond-haired man replied, "Yes, as a matter of fact I am."

The Elder telling the story looked at me with a big grin and said, "Always remember not to be so quick to judge things around you. Sometimes the things we see aren't what we think they are. Always take the time to see the whole picture, not just what you want to see."

He went on to say how the young people of today all seem to walk around suffering from tunnel vision. They seldom see the big picture when looking at the world. That is why most of the younger generation tend to miss what is happening around them. They are not as stupid as everyone likes to think; they have simply gotten used to seeing the world a certain way and find it difficult to change.

The Elder told me that he thinks it is because they spend far too much time playing those awful video games. They become so used to blocking out everything except what is on the screen that they look at life in the same way. Before he left, the Elder told me to always pay attention when Elders are telling a story, because there is always a moral to what they are telling you, even if they don't tell you what it is. Sometimes they want to see how long it takes you to figure it out.

Another time I was visiting this Elder, he had a young man of about twenty staying with him. He told me that the young man had just broken up with his wife and was going through hard times. The young man's family was afraid he would go out and get drunk or do something even more foolish, so the Elder was asked if he would counsel him for a few days. The Elder agreed and the young man packed some of his clothes and prepared to spend the next few days.

That first day we sat around drinking tea and listening to the Elder talk about his late wife, whom he loved and missed very much. When we were having supper that evening, he told the young man and me to always remember one thing: if we ever claim to love someone, we can never hate that person, even later in life. He said if we do end up hating them, it wasn't really love, it was lust. I found myself thinking about that statement for years after the old man had passed on. These were not just empty words; there is an awful lot of truth to them.

Whenever I think about the number of Elders who have passed away in the last year, it saddens me. We are losing them at such a high rate that it makes me think that before long we will not have any of our teachers left. We will become like some of the other cultural groups who are forced to turn to the internet in hopes of finding their culture and teachings. Unfortunately, a lot of our history and culture was not written down, because our people did not do that sort of thing.

This would mean that we would be forced to depend on the white man's version of history. Most of the things regarding First Nations people that have been placed on the internet do not come from First Nations people. Most of this information comes from the professors who have become the so-called experts on Indigenous studies. If we want to avoid this, it is up to the younger generation to ensure that these ways are not lost or forgotten. Once more we must all step up and consider the old teaching, which says we are responsible for the next seven generations.

As residential school survivors we must not allow ourselves to sit back and say that we have lost our cultural and spiritual teachings thanks to those awful schools and the people who ran them. That part might very well carry a lot of truth but placing blame will not bring any of these teachings back to us or to our people. We must be willing to stand up and say, "I will not allow this to happen anymore," and move on. This means that we must be willing to pick up the torch and continue with it. It is up to each one of us to do their part if we still want to have a culture to call our own.

My generation must start by telling ourselves that we are not children anymore, so no one is going to wash our mouths out with soap for speaking about these things ever again. Finally, we can say that we are going to do whatever we can to learn all the teachings that were denied us as children. Then we will be able to do our part in passing them on to the next seven generations. We must stand tall and show the world that the residential school system did not defeat us enough to make us give up who we are or scare us away from relearning all our sacred teachings.

No matter where I go today, if I come across an Elder or a group of Elders, I will take the time to stop by and sit for a while, even if it is just to introduce myself and ask them how they are doing. Although I no longer smoke cigarettes, I always carry a pack or a pouch of tobacco with me for such an occasion. I was always told to present an Elder with tobacco as a sign of respect, even if it is just a few cigarettes. This lets them know you are sincere and have some knowledge of the teachings.

Sometimes I will take the time to tell them about my people or offer a story and ask them what they think of it. Before long they too are sharing stories from their territory. Other times I can be lucky enough to hear a song or two. That is why I always try to carry a hand drum with me, especially when I find myself near one of the local Friendship Centres or any other place where our people gather to spend time with one another.

No matter where I have been in North America, I have noticed that First Nations people are pretty much the same no matter what tribe or area of the country they come from. We are all very social toward one another and will share whatever we have. Whenever you visit with them, they offer you the best seat in the house as well as the best food they have, even if it is just a little bit. This is a habit I learned early from my own grandparents.

Native people, regardless of whether they know one another or not, will acknowledge each other, even in passing. Sometimes it is just a simple nod or smile, but we never ignore another Native person. This is something that most non-Native people have difficulty grasping. They cannot comprehend why we would bother to show love and respect to a person we don't even know, just because they are First Nations.

Not all elderly people I have come across consider themselves Elders in the cultural sense. Over the years I have met quite a few people who will told me they were "senior citizens," not Elders. These are usually residential school survivors who do not consider themselves worthy of the title *Elder*, because they say they do not possess the teachings that would qualify them as teachers in the community. Some will tell you how it was all taken away from them, and even apologize as though they have done something wrong to deserve what happened to them. When this happens, I tell them that I understand, because I am a survivor also. Then we will talk about our personal experiences.

Sometimes you will see these same people sitting in small groups sharing drinks on a park bench or staggering down the street from one bar to another. This is the only time you will hear them trying to sing the songs they heard somewhere over the years, maybe even songs they heard as a child. Sadly, you will often see the younger people laughing at them and telling them to shut up and go home, even referring to them as nothing more than an embarrassment to our people.

When I was a small child still living on the reservation, I remember one of my aunts telling us that it was considered bad luck to laugh at or mock any elderly person, even if they were not from the First Nations community. We were told this kind of behaviour would come back on us in some negative way, so we tried our best to always be respectful toward the older people around us. When they spoke, we did our best to be quiet, even when they weren't speaking to us. If we were playing near them, we would do so as quietly as possible and talk in whispers.

That same aunt told me that when she was a young girl people had such respect for their Elders that they took care of them without question. When they saw an elderly person walking down the street carrying something, they would automatically get up and offer to help with whatever they were carrying—they did not wait to be asked. When an Elder walked into a café and ordered something, even a cup of coffee, someone would get up and go pay for the order. This was how much our people respected the elderly members of the community back then, not like today, when no one finds the time to look out for them.

My aunt said she can remember going places with her parents as a child and coming across Elders out in the community. The first thing her parents always did was ask the Elder if they were all right and if they needed help with anything. Often, they would end up carrying the Elder's groceries to their car or walking them to their vehicle, so they did not slip and fall.

This was a time when most of our people still lived by the Seven Sacred Teachings and followed a set of values that were often compared to the white man's Ten Commandments. These were the Ten Sacred Values given to us by the Creator: respect, cooperation, gratitude, spirituality, honesty, humility, compassion, inclusion and belonging, kindness and bravery. These are the same values that are taught by most of the Aboriginal communities around the world.

The front entrance to Marieval Indian School just prior to its destruction in 1999 to make way for newer school buildings.

Chapter 7

Along with Holistic Healing and the Seven Sacred Teachings, most First Nations people also attribute their spiritual beliefs to the teachings from the Medicine Wheel. These teachings have been around since time immemorial. Passed on from generation to generation through word of mouth, these sacred teachings can be found throughout Turtle Island.

The Medicine Wheel represents our cycle of life from conception to return to the Spirit World. It is a guide to learning, a mentor to help us in our prayers, a counsellor in helping us to better understand ourselves and the world around us, and a constant reminder of our duties and responsibilities as spiritual people walking our path upon Mother Earth. The Medicine Wheel is seen as a way of constantly learning about who we are and how we can in turn relate in a positive way to every living thing that resides upon Mother Earth.

The concept of circles has always been an important part of everyday life for First Nations people here on Turtle Island. Our camps were always built in a circle. When we constructed our homes, they were most often in a circular pattern, such as tepees and hogans. All our most sacred ceremonies are conducted in a circle. The sweat lodges, Sacred Circle ceremonies, pipe ceremonies.... these are all conducted in a circle.

We dance in a circle at the Pow-wows and around the sacred Sundance pole. Our big drums represent the circle. When we sit in council, we form a circle, so everyone is equal, with an equal voice. When Elders teach, they will draw the young people around them in a circle.

First Nations people see life as a continuous circle from birth all the way to death and back to rebirth. We understand that we, like the seasons, pass through several phases as the circle of life and time pass around us. To fall out of this circle is to fall out of harmony with life and to cease to grow and learn as the Creator meant for us to do.

It is for these reasons that the Medicine Wheel, along with the circle teachings, can be used as a positive tool for helping any of our troubled relatives, who sometimes find themselves in conflict with the world around them. These teachings often help to guide these troubled individuals back to the spiritual circle of life, or the Red Road.

We enter the circle at birth, and throughout our journey around the circle, we grow and learn—to stay at any one point on the circle of life is to become static. To become static is to stop growing and if we cannot grow, we stop the life force of our being. This means that our circle comes to an end, and we move to the Spirit World. According to the teachings it is then up to the grandfathers to decide whether you will be sent back to begin a new life circle.

The centre of the Medicine Wheel is movement and change. For those who remain in balance and harmony with all living things, Mother Earth becomes a wonderful place, full of beauty, peace of mind, sharing, contentment, learning, and spiritual growth. However, the instant we allow ourselves to become out of balance, to stray away from the teachings, we become alone and afraid, and feel unloved, unworthy, and rejected. This all leads to depression and anger, and acts of violence against ourselves and others.

It is important to remember that these Medicine Wheel teachings have been around for hundreds upon hundreds of years. Despite this fact, the teachings are the same today as they were all those years ago. Although the First Nations people did not put any of these teachings down in written form, they were still passed on verbally from one generation to the next. Most of our modern-day Elders still prefer to sit down with groups of young people to share these teachings, just like their ancestors did.

There are more than one set of Medicine Wheel teachings, depending on what part of Turtle Island your people come from. Most of the sacred teachings are the same, with slight variations such as the colours that represent each direction. This is because each nation has its own set of sacred colours representing each direction.

Although the majority of my teachings have come from the Dakota people of the prairie provinces, I have always tried to be open-minded. I was always told to respect the people whose territory you are visiting. When it comes to teachings, take the things you feel comfortable with and leave the rest.

I have decided to follow the Medicine Wheel teachings that I feel most comfortable with. These come from an Elder who follows Northern Cree and Dakota teachings. I find his to be the easiest to understand and practice. They are not that much different from the teachings I grew up with. Just remember that no teaching is bad if it helps even one person change his lifestyle and return to the Red Road.

Each direction of our Medicine Wheel represents specific areas of life that are important to us if we want to live in a way that reflects the sacred teachings of our ancestors, beginning with the east, which is represented in yellow. The east is the beginning, the start of a new day, new hope. As the sun rises on this new day, all things are possible. It promises fresh starts. Yellow represents the rising sun.

The Spirit Keeper for this direction is the eagle. Because of its ability to fly so high, the old ones considered the eagle to be closest to the Spirit World. Its ability to reach such great heights led the old ones to believe it could see everything at once, and therefore should represent understanding, the ability for us to understand people and actions outside of our control.

The east also represents spring, the rebirth of Mother Earth. It is the time we pray for Mother Earth, for her healing. To support our life upon her, Mother Earth must remain in balance. It is the turtle that represents Mother Earth, and for this reason Mother Earth is also referred to as "Turtle Island." The turtle is strong and, when left in its natural environment, long-lived, but if turned on its back it becomes weak and will soon die. Just as Mother Earth is long-lived and strong enough to support all living things upon her if left in her natural state, she will also become weak and unable to sustain life if misused.

East represents the physical part of our growth and the wonder of childhood. For most Indigenous people, youth is when everything is new and fresh. Young people can spend hours looking at a baby bird or staring at the stars. They are closest to the Creator, having just come from the Spirit World. They see things clearly; they are not blinded by life's wounds or hardships. They have no notion of the limitations of time, and death is an unknown to them. To the young, each moment, the now, is the important thing in life. They are still in awe of all that they see and learn. They are trusting, loving, and full of *whys*. That is why it is important to protect, encourage, and support this child. Later in our life, this will become known as the "inner child," and it can be a positive influence on the adult, allowing us to still have the ability to learn and grow. If mistreated, it is still the inner child in the adult, but it now becomes negative and destructive.

It is at this point in the Medicine Wheel that we examine the child within us, looking at our past, our childhood, and relationships at that time, seeing how these things impact our present life. We work at healing that child so it can become a positive influence on our life today. We look into the future at our relationships with the young people who will enter our life and what we can contribute to their positive growth. So begins our sacred journey on the Medicine Wheel. Each morning we start our daily smudge and pray to understand and grow from the teachings of the eastern door.

Next on the Medicine Wheel is the south. This direction is represented in black. Some people prefer to use navy blue, depending on which part of Turtle Island they come from. The Spirit Keepers for this direction are the little brother mouse and the coyote. It is in this direction that we also pay honour and respect to all of the grandfathers and grandmothers.

Little brother mouse is living so close to the ground that he can only see within his own small world. Most of the time we are no different than him. It is for this reason that we associate self-awareness, seeking to understand our self with the mouse. We seek to walk in our own truth by recognizing our weaknesses and strengths. We begin to understand what pushes our buttons and why. This is also the time we ask ourselves how we can become healthy in all areas of our life and live in a good and positive way like the Creator intended.

The coyote, who is sometimes referred to as "the trickster," teaches us through experiences outside of ourselves, but which cause us to react in different ways. We ask the people who come to us for advice or direction to think back and remember a time when something looked good to them and they wanted it with their whole being, would do anything to have it, only to have their wish fulfilled and to learn that the very thing they desired the most was also the thing that caused them the most hurt and pain.

It is in this way that the coyote teaches us to be careful when we look at a person, situation, or activity, teaching us that we need to examine all sides thoroughly before we make hasty decisions. He is also teaching us how to truly get to know ourselves in order to know what will complete us and make us happy in the end. Coyote is much more than just a trickster.

The south also represents midday, which is the time for us to sit back and look at our morning and how we have spent it. It is also the time when we remove any negativity we may have accumulated throughout our morning and deal with any issues we have faced. When we are done with this, we can fully commit our afternoon and evening to positive things.

It is the time that we concentrate on summer, a time of growing and fulfillment, coming to fruit from our childhood years. This is the time of our emotional growth. We are now praying for those between the ages of twenty and forty. This is also the time we start forming and following our own standards, goals, and values. We are becoming what everyone around us considers to be adults, with our own thoughts and beliefs about life and family.

We develop adult relationships and fall in love. We decide on and start working on our future careers. At this time, we have begun to experience some of the hardships of life. We are learning and growing, becoming the full person that we will eventually become. We are busy with our life, our families, and our careers, just as Mother Earth is busy producing the fruits of her labour. Our life is full, and we often do not take the time to consider what is beyond this period. *Now* is the important thing—doing, achieving, and forming our future.

Emotionally this is one of the hardest times in any person's life: falling in love, determining our own inner worth, and watching our children come into the world, grow, then begin their journey away from our protection. Facing the disappointments of life, determining our weaknesses and strengths, and learning to adjust to this knowledge.

The delicate butterfly represents this emotional growth as it flutters first here then there, always in motion, always seeking. Father Sun represents the height of our physical self, the strong rays of our life force. It is the feminine side within us that resides here, giving us the ability to love, to share, and to care, to be compassionate to others, to heal our own wounds and the hurts of those we love and care for. We gather all into the comfort of her being.

We all need the strong woman within us. It is this part of us that allows us to nurture our families and be compassionate in our relationships, to care about the world around us, to give and receive with gentleness and kindness. The woman within gives us our artistic talents, expressing our deepest emotional self. It is important to keep the woman within us in balance. When this side of us becomes weak, it generally leads to lack of feelings and compassion. In weakness we easily give in to negativity and turn away from our path in hopelessness and helplessness.

Remember to always honour the grandfathers and grandmothers in this sacred direction. They are the teachers, the givers of their wisdom and life experiences for those who would take the time to listen and learn. As we walk in the path of those who have gone before us, we begin to understand what they have gone through and to learn from our own life experiences, so that one day we too can pass these experiences on to our grandchildren.

In the Medicine Wheel teachings in this direction, we examine the feminine side that exists within all of us. We look closely at the female relationships in our lives, what positive and negative effects they have had. We look at our ability or lack thereof to form lasting and positive relationships, and what we can do in the future to correct our weaknesses and bring strength to this area of our life.

Next on the Medicine Wheel we look to the west, which is represented in red. To the west we find the Medicine Bear, who is the keeper of our spiritual life. The old ones say it is the Medicine Bear who taught us how to find the medicines to heal our self. Red represents the setting sun. It is now evening, the time when our workday is closing. Here our struggles have been identified; we have reached a point of change in our life. We pray for those between the ages of forty and sixty. We have been busy growing physically, fighting for our careers, raising our families, establishing lasting relationships. We are what we have made ourselves at this time.

There is still time for growth, learning, and wisdom, but we are also aware that time is running out, and often we find there is an emptiness we are unable to identify, a longing for something more, an awareness that our time on Mother Earth is limited. We look toward our spirituality in new terms, in the understanding that we will soon be facing the Creator and the Spirit World.

It is a time to look closely at our life, a last chance, if you will, to correct our weaknesses. Through our spirituality we judge our past, present, and future. It is autumn and Mother Earth is preparing for the winter to come. The hardest labour is behind us; there is now time to consider our future as spiritual people.

We have finished our physical growth, reached the peak of our mental growth, and now we can examine our life with intelligence and vision. Where are we going from here? The frog represents the water, and the water is the healing and cleansing agent, allowing us to clean away the negative from our life and concentrate fully on preparing ourselves for the time to come. Grandmother Moon is high in the night sky, reminding us that our day on Mother Earth is almost finished. It is time to start closing the circle of our life.

In the west stands the warrior within us. The one who, when we are walking our life path in a good and positive way, stands up for the truths we believe in, protects all of those we love and care for, and gives us the strength to pass through the tough times. When we walk our path in a negative manner, the warrior becomes out of balance. Violence against oneself and others is the only outcome of being out of balance on your spiritual path. One must always be aware of his or her thoughts and actions to avoid straying from the path.

In the Medicine Wheel teachings, we look closely at the warrior within us. When he walks a negative path, many around him will suffer. We look at the male relationships in our past and identify the negative and positive values that came from each of them. We look at our own life and try to identify where the warrior within has failed, and where he has succeeded. We begin to find positive ways to keep the warrior within us strong, and we learn to use this newfound strength for constructive purposes.

As we prepare for an evening of relaxation, we take the time to face west with our smudge and ask the Creator to bring us spiritual peace in all areas of our life, and to give us a better understanding of the sacred teachings that come from this direction. We now understand the importance of these sacred teachings.

Finally, before we go to sleep at night, after the cares of the day are behind us, we turn to the north. White represents the north, and the winter snows. The sacred buffalo, the giver of food, shelter, medicine, and all good things, is the Spirit Keeper for this sacred direction.

The north is the last point of our daily journey. We are now in the winter of our life, and just as Mother Earth has covered herself with snow to rest and restore herself for the coming of new season, we also prepare ourselves for rest from this world and the coming of a new life. We have walked through the storms of our age. If we have learned and followed the teachings and are in balance and harmony with all living things, then we have walked through the fire and joined our spirits with the Thunderbird in preparation for our flight home. If we have learned by our life experiences and the teachings of our Elders, we are now entering a time of true wisdom, which we in turn will share with others. We are now becoming the Elders.

Now is the time we look back to see and understand the legacy we have left behind. Are we proud of what we have accomplished, or do we live in shame and dissatisfaction? Has our testing, while we walked through the fire of life, left us an inner child who remains in awe at all the Creator has provided? Does the woman within remain caring and strong? Is the warrior satisfied that he has done all that was required of him? It is in the true answer to these questions that we can define our legacy.

In wisdom we accept that we have not always been perfect. We have hurt others and ourselves along the way. We have not always done our best with the gifts the Creator has so generously given to us. However, if we can honestly say we have done our best at each point in the Medicine Wheel, that we tried, then our legacy will live on in a good and positive way.

As this day slowly comes to a close, we quietly give thanks by finishing with our final smudge before sleep. We not only ask the Creator to give us wisdom in our daily life, but to protect us as we sleep. This is when we ask him to grant us peaceful dreams that we may awaken refreshed and ready for the next day, to help us learn from the mistakes of this day and to guide and protect us in the coming day.

Group of younger children celebrating the Canadian Centennial in 1967. This group included my younger brother Max.

Chapter 8

As First Nations people we have to continue to remind ourselves daily that none of us have the right to judge others. That is solely the Creator's job, and when the time comes for you to stand in front of him, he will ask you what you did with the gift he gave you, meaning the life that you had. Then it will be up to you to explain why you spent your life foolishly thinking that you had the right to label and judge others around you.

The Elders are constantly telling us that it is up to each of us to live our lives to the best of our abilities. Then when we end up in the Spirit World, we can say we tried our best to help those around us, and we did our best to take care of Mother Earth and all the wonderful things she provides for us.

If we can honestly say we have lived up to these things, we are living as the Creator intended us to live. Those of us who cannot say this will have a much harder time getting into that wonderful place the Creator has waiting for us.

As human beings we often make mistakes, and we sometimes do things we know are wrong, but we also have the ability to learn from those mistakes and never make them again. I remember being told that if someone says they are sorry for something they did, or tells you they made a mistake, you have to accept them at their word and forgive them for making that simple mistake. This goes along with the Seven Sacred Teachings.

However, if they turn around and do the same thing to you a second time, it is not a mistake, it is on purpose. I have always believed that the point this teaching is trying to make is that everyone deserves a second chance, so I try my hardest to live by that simple philosophy. Sometimes this can become quite difficult, because when I find myself becoming overly frustrated with someone I often want to walk away and say, "No one ever bothered to give *me* a second chance in life."

Thankfully, these feelings don't happen often, but sometimes I find myself getting caught up in that old "poor me" way of thinking that dominated my life for so many years. Usually, I am feeling sorry for myself because things did not go the way I anticipated. Whenever any of these negative feelings begin to creep back into my daily thinking, I remind myself that this only proves one thing: that I am no different than anyone else.

Most times I am lucky enough that these feelings are only fleeting and never last for more than a few minutes. Other times, I go to one of my Elders and talk about the problems before they get too far out of hand and start taking control of my thoughts and emotions. I must constantly remind myself of why I am doing these things, and I must keep telling myself I do not want to go back to the old lifestyle that I fought so long and hard to get away from.

The one thing that I try hard to keep in mind is that I must not say anything as long as I am feeling any of these negative emotions, because my mind is not seeing things clearly at times like this. I will tell myself that I honestly do not want to make myself look foolish by saying something I know I will only end up regretting later. I find it helps if I remind myself of the times in my past when I said or did things, I ended up regretting for days.

When it starts to get tough, I remind myself of the simple fact that words are sharp, and they have the ability to hurt others deeply. Remembering how some of the things that were said to me as a child affected me for years is enough to cause me to hang my head and feel badly for the people I hurt with my foolish words. I tell myself that I am the only one responsible for what comes out of my mouth, so it is up to me alone to censor those words.

My grandmother once told me that words are the one thing in life that can never be taken back. Once you release them, they are out there for eternity. One careless word spoken in haste can forever change someone's opinion of you. Even if people tell you they forgive you for something you may have said earlier in anger, they will always be carrying it somewhere in the back of their mind. Then, just when you start to think that everything is back to normal, they will remind you of your momentary lapse of judgement. So always be careful of what comes out of your mouth, because in the end you own those words.

I attended a cultural camp being put on by a group of Elders to try to bring some of the troubled youth back to their own culture. The camp went on for approximately eight hours a day and lasted for ten days. Throughout each day, various Elders would get up and take their turn sharing some of their personal experiences and teachings.

One Elder told the young people in attendance that they should never speak negatively about another person no matter what they have done to you. When you do this, you are shedding negativity on more people than you realize. Sometimes these are people you care about.

He told them that everything they do or say reflects not only on them, but on their family and its teachings. When an Elder sees younger people misbehaving, the first thing they do is ask, "Where do they come from?" and "Who are their people?" Then they will ask who the Elders of that family are. Sometimes you will hear them say this young person had a poor upbringing, meaning the Elders in that family did a poor job of teaching them right from wrong. That is why we always have to think before we act. Someone is always watching, even when we do not think so.

He told me that when he was their age, his grandfather told him the only time anyone could speak badly about another person was after they have stood up in front of everyone in the community and told them everything negative about themselves. This meant he would have to stand up and tell everyone who would listen about all the terrible things he had ever done in his lifetime. It meant sharing all the deep dark secrets he was hiding in his closet, the things he wanted no one to know about.

His grandfather told him that when he had completed all of this, no one would ever be able to fault him for speaking badly about another person. Then the Elder who was speaking to the group laughed and said that, as far as most people are concerned, this is too high a price to pay, so maybe we should all just learn how to keep all those negative thoughts and words to ourselves. This way we do not risk making a fool of ourselves either.

When someone starts talking negatively about another person, it is up to all of us to speak up and stop the gossip. We have to say as politely as possible that we do not want to hear that sort of talk. Sometimes we just have to tell the person talking that this is none of our business, so we don't want to know.

The Elder told everyone about the importance of prayer, and once again he reminded us, we should always pray for people we are having any kind of conflict with. This, he said, was the one teaching that cannot be emphasised enough. He wanted everyone there to understand we would only receive the things we needed in life by praying for other people, even people we do not know. This is all part of being humble and able to show the Creator you can place the needs of other people before your own.

He informed the group that one of the easiest ways to avoid disappointment was by keeping our wants and needs the same. Whenever you tell yourself that you want something, stop, and ask yourself, *is it really something I cannot do without, or is it just something I want to own because it might make my life easier?* Wanting something for the sake of having it does not mean you *need* it. To truly *need* something would mean your life or someone you love is in danger if you do not have it.

He told everyone we should always begin our days with prayer and end it the same way. Every morning when we wake up, the first thing we should be doing is giving thanks to the Creator for everything he has provided for us. First, thank him for the beautiful day he has given us; whether the sun is shining or not, it is still beautiful. Thank him for all the medicines and the animals he has provided to feed and clothe us, so we may live, and do not forget to thank him for the family and relatives who are there to love us. Remember that he is the one who provides us with these things every day of our lives.

Then the Elder told everyone that it is possible for a person to pray every day for things to get better and nothing will ever change. It all depends on how sincere our prayers are. When we are truly grateful for the things we have in our lives right now, even if the things are small in the eyes of others, and the Creator sees that we are sincerely grateful, he will give us the changes that we so desperately require in life. Remember that he does not always give us what we want; sometimes he gives us what we need.

Before the Elder closed the gathering with a prayer, he told the group a short story about learning to be humble. His story was about two men sitting down to pray together. One of the men was young and carried an elaborate and fancy prayer bundle with the nicest of beadwork and the prettiest eagle feathers. When he was done laying out his sacred objects on his new star blanket, there were fancy carved rattles, drums, and pipes with beautiful carvings on them. He had the finest medicines and a nice, big, shiny abalone shell to use as a smudge bowl. Even the spotted eagle wing with its beaded handle he used for a fan was magnificent.

The old man beside him began laying out his old and weathered pipe with a single badly aged hawk feather, and an old eagle fan that looked as ancient as the elderly man. He only had the sparsest of medicines, and as he began making his prayer ties for the ceremony the younger man chuckled to himself, because the old man's tobacco was so dry that it almost blew away in the slight afternoon breeze. Despite this, the old man quietly filled his pipe.

When the two men were finished praying and had put their prayer bundles away, the old man stood up and gracefully thanked the younger man for his prayers and prepared to leave. All the people taking part in the ceremony crowded around the old man and presented him with tobacco and other gifts as a way of saying thank you for conducting the sacred ceremony, something not unusual for the people to do following any ceremonial gathering.

The younger man began wondering why no one was showing him the same respect and gratitude they were showing to the old man. *After all, I have a much nicer bundle*, he told himself. He went on telling himself these people probably feel pity for this foolish old man. With that, he shrugged his shoulders and prepared to leave the gathering.

When the story was over, the Elder asked everyone one final question before allowing them to leave. He asked everyone in a very serious tone, "Whose prayers do you think the Creator paid more attention to? Was it the young man who was like a flashy young peacock strutting his stuff to impress everyone in attendance, or was it the old man who did his best with what were obviously well-used regalia from an ancient bundle that had all but served its purpose in life?"

People who do not know any better would quickly say the younger man, because his things were new and flashy. However, wiser people would point out that the old man has well-used regalia thanks to years of practice. He has knowledge and his prayers are more likely to be straight from the heart, but most important was the fact that the old man was not trying to impress anyone with what he had or how he did things, he was just praying in the best way he could with what he had.

The Elder's story caries a strong message to those who will listen carefully with an open mind. It tells us all we should stop trying to outdo everyone else all the time and concentrate on doing the best job we can with whatever the Creator has provided for us at that place and time.

This story always helps me to remember those Seven Sacred Teachings that our spirituality is based upon. If we do our best to not only remember those teachings, but to live by them as well, we will not end up like the young man and look like nothing more than a show-off. Anytime an Elder is telling a story, do your best to listen and you will see that there is always an important message hidden in that story, one that will help you at another point in your life.

When I was younger, I did not place much emphasis on these stories, believing they were simply another way of entertaining each other. When I began working closely with the Elders, I was informed that through these stories our people were able to keep the teachings alive. During the days when our teachings were outlawed and many people were sent to jail for practicing the old ways, it was through these stories that the Elders were able to secretly keep our culture alive.

Our ancestors never considered trying to put things down in the form of written history simply because our people were nomadic. They had to move with the different seasons to obtain food and everything else that was necessary for the survival of the community. I remember one of the Elders laughing and saying, "Could you imagine carrying all those books when it came time to move the camp? They would have no room for anything else."

That is why older people patiently spend hours telling children the same stories over and over, both as a way of entertaining them and as a way of passing on the knowledge, so that the culture and spirituality will not die. The grandparents watch to see what kind of things interest the child, and they decide what sort of teachings to pass on. This is how they determine what your role will be when you became an adult and are expected to take your place in the community circle. If you become good at something, you are encouraged to work with certain Elders who are fluent in your field of interest.

Chapter 9

When I was first out of the residential school system, I was leery of Native spirituality because of the negative teachings imposed on us by the Church. I was always told that my ancestors were devil worshipers who practiced nothing more than witchcraft or black magic. This led me to believe there were all sorts of evil spirits involved in our spiritual practices, similar to the voodoo that is often portrayed in movies about the Black people in the southern part of the United States.

Because of the mixed-up views held by the Church, I was always hesitant about discussing any of the spiritual experiences I had gone through. This included the vivid dreams and visions I was given during my participation in Vision Quest ceremonies over the years. I was afraid to talk about these things because I did not want anyone accusing me of being crazy or of having hallucinations.

The longer I worked with my Elders and spiritual advisors, the more I began experiencing these "spiritual events," as I have come to call them. At first, I tried to play them off as coincidence, or just my overactive imagination. When I finally found the courage to talk to one of the Elders about these things, I was told not to worry. He told me this was a good sign, and that the longer I followed these ways and practice the ceremonies, the stronger I would become spiritually. I was told that everyone who follows these ways long enough, in a sincere manner, begins to experience things like this.

These experiences just mean that the grandfathers are starting to recognize you and they are beginning to acknowledge you for your participation. Eventually the grandfathers will show you many different things and maybe even pass on gifts in the form of knowledge or medicines. When I experience something like this, I was told to take the time to stop and say a short prayer of thanks and appreciation, acknowledging the Creator and giving thanks to the grandfathers and grandmothers for allowing me to be a part of the experience and the teaching.

At first these incidents seemed supernatural and left me wondering whether I had witnessed the event. I was told many times never to be afraid and to always be humble and respectful toward the spirits, so I always prayed and accepted what I saw, even if I was left confused. I told myself that when the time was right, the Creator would allow me to understand what happened, and until then I just needed to be patient.

My first spiritual encounter happened when I was participating in a crowded sweat lodge ceremony in Prince Albert, Saskatchewan, with the other participants of that year's Vision Quest ceremony. By this time, I was well into my Healing Journey and had already participated in a lot of previous sweat lodge ceremonies with these same people. I knew each of them well.

On this day I was sitting in the southern doorway and finding the lodge unusually hot. My shoulders and the tips of my ears were beginning to burn, almost to the point that I wanted to scream. I was beginning to question whether I had the strength to finish the round. Just when I was about to holler for the door, I began to feel as though something was moving quickly around my head and shoulders, from one side to the other. I had a crazy feeling that something was thoroughly looking me over. When I felt it stop directly in front of my face, I closed my eyes and held them tightly shut, too afraid to even consider peeking.

I began to pray harder, just the way I had been taught by my Elders. I was not sure what I had just experienced, but I thanked the grandfathers for acknowledging me with their presence and asking them to forgive me for being scared. Part of me was afraid to open my eyes for fear of what I might see. Without realizing it, I had forgotten all about how hot it was earlier, and my ears were no longer burning.

My mind was now racing, but the sound of water being splashed onto the rocks brought me back. When I opened my eyes, I was surprised to see what appeared to be an orange ball floating there, directly across the pit from me. It was at chest level with my sweat lodge brother Norm, who had his eyes closed and was praying. I could tell this because, to my amazement, the light coming from the orange ball was so bright that I could see everyone in the lodge clearly, including Norm's face, which was being lit up so brightly I wondered why he could not notice the light in front of him. I could even see his eyelids flicker as he moved his eyes around.

When the round was over and the Elder called for the door, I was still in a state of astonishment and confusion. I noticed the Elder looking at me with a huge grin on his face, and I thought to myself that he had to know something was happening with me. He asked me if I had "seen that too." Without saying anything, I shook my head, indicating I had. When he asked me what colour it was, I felt much better, because I knew I had not been imagining things. After all, two people couldn't possibly imagine the same thing at the same time, at least not that I was aware of.

When the ceremony was over, the Elder told me this was why he always told everyone to keep their eyes open, even in the sweat lodge, because the grandfathers might decide they are going to show you something, and you will miss it if you are not paying attention to what is going on around you. Always try to be in the moment and you will never miss out on anything that life has to show you. Even if it is totally dark inside the sweat lodge, you must always expect the unexpected.

Many years later I was at an Aboriginal healing lodge called Kwikwexwelhp in the Fraser Valley of British Columbia when I had a similar experience. On a clear night in early October, just after the first snow had fallen, I was out walking with three other residents of the lodge. It was somewhere around 10:00 p.m. and it was dark enough outside to see the stars clearly. We were slowly walking along one of the back roads, sharing stories from our childhoods and pointing out all the different constellations we had come to know, when a light appeared some twenty feet in front of us.

This time the light I experienced was pale blue and appeared to slowly come down the side of the hill bordering the road. As it crossed over the gravel road and went through the heavy brush heading off toward the nearby creek, everything around us become eerily quiet.

At first, we were all stunned at what we head seen, and of course everyone began trying to find some way to justify what they had witnessed. At first, I wanted to speak up and tell them about the first time I experienced this type of phenomenon, but I decided not to say anything. I kept quiet and listened to what everyone else had to say.

One of the guys said that, at first, he thought it was the light from someone's cell phone. Everyone laughed and asked what anyone would be doing walking around in the dark with nothing but the light from their phone? Besides, someone else added, there was absolutely no noise coming from the direction of the light, which was only about twenty feet in front of us. If a person came down the side of the mountain and crossed over the road to go down the other side, we would have heard something, especially with all the gravel and dead leaves that covered the area.

The next day one of the local Elders from the long house on the nearby Chehalis Indian Band stopped by to visit with everyone. One of the guys I was walking with the night before began telling him what we saw, and to my surprise the Elder knew exactly what we were describing to him. He told us that what we had seen was a spirit form, one of the many that inhabit that area of the territory.

The Elder told us that we should go back to that spot, or as close to it as possible, and make an offering of food or tobacco, because these spirits do not show themselves to just anyone who happens to come along. He told us stories of how different people who were camped up there picking berries and gathering medicine claimed to have seen up to a dozen of these coloured lights floating down the nearby creek, sometimes in a nice, even row. Sometimes these same people would tell of hearing drumming and singing as the lights floated by. He said this is how some people receive the old songs.

The area where this healing lodge was built is considered to be very spiritual by the nearby Chehalis people, whose Indian band was just down the mountain from the site. There was a large freshwater creek running through the area that was fed by melting snow from the mountains that surrounded the area. It was the perfect spot to set up camp if you needed. This became a regular gathering place for the Chehalis people long ago when they were out looking for food and gathering medicines. They say the name "Kwikwexwelhp" means "a place to gather medicines."

When dealing with spiritual matters of any sort, I often find it difficult to speak about the things I have experienced due to the considerable number of skeptics out there, even amongst our own people. Whenever someone shares stories like this, there is usually one or two people who will start talking about evil spirits, or what they like to call "bad medicine." Most often these are the unfortunate people whose lives have been dominated and changed by the residential school system or one of the many churches.

The Elders are always telling me that these people are once again being influenced by the Church and its stories about good and evil, God against the devil. Our people do not believe in the devils or demons any more than we believe in angels. In fact, the idea of evil is uniquely a human concept. When we look around at the animal kingdom, it is clear they do not see themselves as good or evil when they kill for survival. They are only feeding themselves and their young. Only humans are capable of understanding the difference between good and evil.

Elders will always tell you there cannot be one without the other. There must be evil in order for there to be good. They tell us there has to be balance in all areas of life for the universe to function properly. When we think about it, everything has an opposite. Male and female, hot and cold, light and dark, big and small.... this is how the Creator made the universe and all that it contains. As human beings we tend to try to analyze everything around us. These things were not put there for us to try to understand. Sometimes they are there for us to simply accept and give thanks for.

I was told by many Elders over the years to be vigilant and careful of the people and the ceremony I am thinking of taking part in. They told me that people are not always what or who they portray themselves to be. These individuals are what everyone in the Aboriginal community refer to as "popcorn Elders." They do not really have experience doing any of the ceremonies, they are just trying to mimic what they have seen elsewhere. Following these people can have tragic results, because they are playing with things, they have no understanding of. We must all remember to respect and fear the Spirit World just enough to not play around with anything pertaining to this area.

My Elders have always told me to avoid people who claim to know things, as well as people who walk around making claims, they have been given certain powers. This kind of person can hurt you and your loved ones. Always remember that true medicine people do not ever make claims about who they are or what they can do. They never claim to have powers. They will tell you they are plain men, and the Creator is the only one who has any kind of power.

The real medicine people rely on word of mouth to lead the people to them. They always say that when you are meant to know, the Creator will lead you to the right person. That is why I always tell people to pray about it and then leave it in the Creator's hands. When the time is right, the answers will come to you. However, you have to honestly believe in the Creator and in the power of your prayers.

Since starting my Healing Journey, there have been a number of people I have been warned about. When I mentioned the names of these people, someone with knowledge would say, "Get yourself away from that one, because they are not really what they are claiming to be." This is when I would say a prayer for that person and move on without showing any disrespect.

Sometimes these are people who claim to be knowledgeable, but really are not. Some of these people get their teachings off the internet, or from books. They have never actually been to a Sundance or any other significant ceremony for themselves. They just preach about the things they have been told about by other people. If you pay close attention to what they are trying to tell you, it will become obvious they are frauds. These are the kind of people who can hurt you, so be careful.

Every Elder and spiritual advisor I have chosen to work with over the years has come highly recommended by people who have worked with them in the past. None of these spiritual people needed to advertise and talk about their knowledge or abilities; their reputations are spread by word of mouth. It is not that difficult to find good, knowledgeable people to work with, as long as you are not afraid to do your homework. Do not be afraid to ask questions.

Whether you come from their nation or not is not relevant. Most spiritual people love to teach, and work with anyone who is sincere and willing to learn what they have to offer. They see this as their way of preserving the culture and ensuring it is there for the next seven generations. Most spiritual people see it as their duty to pass on as much of their knowledge as possible. If they cannot continuously do this, they begin to feel that they are failing. Many of the recognized Elders in the community have told me never to be too quick to jump on the bandwagon because someone you meet claims, they are an Elder. I was told more than once to stand back for a while and quietly observe the person from a distance. This allows you to see for yourself how they speak and behave to the people around them. Make them prove they really are what they claim to be. If you like what you see and hear from them, give them your full attention. If you are not sure, or you do not like what you see in the person, walk away, and keep searching for the right one.

This philosophy is no different than the Christians who teach their followers about false prophets trying to lead people away from their path to salvation. This is one teaching I have paid attention to over the past thirty years, and I have never been disappointed with the results. There were many times I walked away from some of these so-called Elders and spiritual advisors, but I always found someone more appropriate to replace them, someone with teachings that were more to my liking.

When I meet someone who claims to have powers, I just smile and tell them, "That's nice." Most of the time these people just give me a strange look before quickly walking away. When that does not work, I tell them I have always been told that we as human beings do not have powers, only the Creator does. We are just plain men and nothing more. If they become offended by this or start to get defensive, they are not the kind of teacher I want to learn from, so I politely excuse myself and walk away.

I have always been careful when it came to choosing my spiritual advisors and Elders. So far, I think I have done a pretty good job of selecting the right ones. The ones I chose were well respected in the community and came highly recommended by people who follow the Red Road. Every one of my teachers comes with a long history of working with individuals like me who are trying to get back to the culture, people who have been lost and are trying to regain their identity. These are people I trust with my life.

This type of scrutinizing is important, because these are the people into whose hands you are going to place your life and wellbeing. These Elders and spiritual advisors are going to place you into situations that can become harmful if they do not know what they are doing. Some of these ceremonies have the potential to cause serious harm to people when not performed in the proper manner. This is why every knowledgeable Elder you meet will always tell you to be careful about whose teachings you choose to follow, because you are placing your life, along with the lives of your loved ones, in that person's hands.

When I first sat down with my Elder and talked about whether I was ready to participate in a Vision Quest, I was told it would require one full year of preparation. He told me I might experience things during this ceremony that will frighten or confuse me. It was explained to me that when someone is participating in this type of ceremony, they are travelling into the Spirit World and seeking the guidance or direction of the spirits. This is a very sacred ceremony that is not to be played with under any circumstance.

I realize that there are still a lot of skeptics out there who do not believe in these ceremonies and will scoff at the idea of people having visions or dreams that are meant to help them or the people around them. I have even had individuals tell me that any time you take food and water away from someone for four days and nights it will naturally cause hallucinations, especially if the individual is fasting in the heat. They do not see anything spiritual in this at all; it is scientific to them. They already have their minds made up, and nothing you do or say is going to change their way of thinking.

These same people are quick to tell me that participating in any of the Sundance ceremonies is the practice of archaic rituals. They think that piercing your chest and hanging from a tree until your skin tears is barbaric. They say that no society or person in their right mind would ever condone such inhumane and barbaric acts of self-mutilation. They say we should not be teaching our children to follow these rituals.

Then they tell me that we as First Nations people need to learn how to change our way of thinking and get with the times, because we are no longer considered uncivilized like our ancestors were. They say these rituals are often the very things that caused the white men to call us pagans in the first place.

I feel sorry for people who think like this, because they are the ones who are truly lost in this world. They are trying as hard as they can to fit into the non-Native society, so they are willing to deny and condemn their own culture to appease their white neighbors. They fail to see that no matter how hard they try to be like their white neighbors, they will never be white. They will always be Aboriginal, and they will always be looked at as outsiders. This sort of thinking is the cause of us slowly losing our identity as a people. One by one, all our cultural teachings are slowly dying out around us, beginning with our languages. We are becoming extinct as a nation or as a people, and it is our own doing. We have to stand up for what we are before it is too late. This may be hard for some of our people to hear, but it is the truth whether we like it or not.

The residential school system took everything away from us and now we are allowing their anti–First Nations teachings and beliefs to negatively influence our lives and values. We must all learn to accept who we are and where we come from before it is too late. This begins by accepting who our ancestors are, then respecting their spiritual and cultural beliefs. Whether we choose to follow or believe any of the teachings of our ancestors is ultimately up to us, but we need to keep these teachings alive for the simple fact that they represent who we are as a people. This is one fact we cannot change.

Despite how strongly I want to bring back my own culture and live my life as a First Nations person, I am forced to accept and adapt to the dominant society every time I leave the reservation. I know that the times are changing around me, but that does not mean I cannot have the best of both worlds. During the day I can enjoy a cappuccino or a McDonald's burger just like anyone else, and still be a proud First Nations man when I go home at the end of the day. To me, being proud does not mean turning my back on progress, it means holding my head high in spite of it, something that took me far too long to understand.

Today I see myself as a proud First Nations person who has learned how to accept the positive changes the white society has introduced to our people. Yes, there were a lot of evil things that were introduced into First Nations communities, but there were also some good things. Realizing this was easier than I first imagined, but as I looked more closely at everything, I realized that none of these things have changed the colour of my skin or what I carry in my heart. Today I certainly do not consider myself to be one of the people who shows up at rallies and screams things like, "Down with white society!" I guess I no longer blame the white man for everything that has gone wrong in the world around me.

I want to instill pride in the younger generation by teaching them First Nations singing and dancing yet tell the kids to learn as much as they can in school, because it will help them establish a good place in society once they are finished. The days of being angry at the world over the residential school system are over for me. It is now time for me to move on in a positive and healthy manner.

We need to instill this kind of thinking into more of our youth to prevent them from getting into so much trouble when they try to fit into the non-Native society around them. Today, many of our First Nations communities are experiencing things like gang violence and teen suicide because our youth are feeling lost and unaccepted. It is often exceedingly difficult for First Nations youth to feel they fit in when they leave the reserve, especially when they have to deal with a society that has such different beliefs and values than we do.

Aboriginal values that are related to the justice system are all based solely on rehabilitation, reconciliation, and healing, while the government's justice system is based on punishment and restitution. They are quick to send people to jail, but with First Nations people it is only after all attempts to rehabilitate the person have failed that we as a community resort to banishment. This was always seen as the ultimate punishment, meant for those deemed beyond help or who simply refused to change for the good of the community.

In the fall of 2011, while I was in Mission, British Columbia, my younger brother passed away due to what I was told were complications related to his diabetes. I found myself unable to make it down to his funeral, which was held on our home reserve, the Cowessess First Nation, where I first attended residential school as a five-year-old. All I could do was pray for his family and send them my condolences, which they accepted. Still, I was left with a heavy heart.

Although my brother and I had not seen each other in over twenty years, we kept in contact regularly by telephone and letters. Therefore, I knew he was not in the best of health for some time prior to his passing. He too had recently returned to the sweat lodge and was becoming a regular participant in the weekly ceremonies back home on the reserve. In one of his last letters, he told me he was thinking about participating in a Sundance sometime in the near future to ask for strength and guidance.

My brother was always an active man in his community and liked to hunt and work on vehicles. When his health began to deteriorate to the point where he could no longer do any of this, I sent him one of my pipes that I had used during my Vision Quest days and told him to learn how to pray with it whenever he was feeling too sick for the sweat lodge. Luckily, there were Elders there who were more than willing to teach him how to use the pipe. Despite all his efforts and prayers, his illness was just too much, and he died nine months later from complications related to his diabetes.

Approximately a month after his passing, I had a dream he came to see me. This was one of those dreams that was so vivid and clear it seemed real. Prior to falling asleep, I was relaxing in my bedroom reading one of the many books by the well-known Lakota Medicine Man, Black Elk. I often read his books when I was feeling down or in need of some spiritual pick me up. On this day I was feeling sorry for myself for not staying closer to the few family members I had gotten to know over the previous few years.

In my dream I was lying in my room reading the book when my brother walked in and looked around. He said he just wanted to see where I was living. As he was talking to me, I recall feeling confused, because I knew he was gone. At the same time, I could not help noticing how vivid and clear everything appeared. I even recall the dust particles floating in the sunbeam that came through the window behind me. As for my brother, he looked just the way I remembered him when we last saw each other some twenty years earlier. It was as though he had not aged a minute in the twenty-odd years that had gone by.

When I awoke, I lay there trying to remember every detail. Then I jumped up excited and went to see my Elder, telling him everything I could recall about the dream. He told me it sounded as though I had been visited by my brother's spirit, so I lit the smudge and said a short prayer acknowledging him. The following week I began to make arrangements with my Elder from the Chehalis Indian Band to hold a burning ceremony in my brother's name. This was to feed his spirit and help him with his journey to the other side. Ceremonies like this are important, because those loved ones who have passed on are counting on us to feed them and help them reach the other side. I found this out during one of my Vision Quest ceremonies back in the early 1990s, when I had a vision that involved me walking down a narrow and well-worn path surrounded by bush. All along the way I kept passing people who were ragged and dirty, all different ages. Some were men and some were women. There were even small children. They were holding their hands out to me as though they were begging me for something.

When the quest was over and I was finally sitting in the sweat lodge talking with my Elders about my vision, they did their best to help me understand what I had seen. They told me this was not something new to them, because other people over the years have experienced nearly identical visions. They told me not to disregard any of what I had seen, because this was meant to show me that the Spirit World is real, and the spirits do exist. Now it was up to me to show them their vision was not a waste, and I would begin doing my part.

The Elders told me all the people who I had passed along that path in my vision were my ancestors who have died and gone to the other side. They were begging me to feed them and make offerings so they could continue their journey to the Spirit World. The Elders than explained to me that if we do not offer food, cloth, and tobacco, they become stuck in limbo and sit along the path, waiting for someone to feed them. I suppose this can be seen as our own form of purgatory, just like the people in the Catholic Church are always talking about.

We must learn to honour our relatives who have gone before us by recognizing them in ceremony. This can be done by simply singing their songs and letting them know they are not forgotten. This is how it has been done for hundreds of years. The Elders told me to try to make offerings at least once a month from then on, and my ancestors will be able to carry on to the Spirit World in a good way.

These stories pertaining to the Spirit World are not something exclusive to First Nations people. Practically every nationality in the world has its own teachings related to the spirits and the Spirit World. A Buddhist person once told me that the Spirit World is the same for everyone, except there are different dimensions that each of us goes to depending on what kind of spiritual beliefs we have practiced throughout our life. I thought about this for the longest time.

The monk told me that people are reborn over and over again until they learn the lessons that are necessary to remain in the afterlife. He told me that people are sometimes reborn five or six times, depending on how long it takes them to learn what they need. He told me that a lot of nationalities believe in reincarnation, including a great number of First Nations tribes throughout North America.

As we talked, he began explaining what happens whenever a person experiences what we have come to know as "déjà vu," or that feeling that we did something already. He explained to me that every one of us has planned our entire life before we are born. We picked out who our parents will be, as well as our nationality.

Whether we choose to have a burning ceremony every year or simply make an offering every time we attend a sweat lodge ceremony is entirely up to us. The important thing is that we are not forgetting about those who have gone on before us. We do this so that when it comes time for us to begin our own journey, we will not have a hard time either. We will be remembered for the things we have done while we were still here amongst the living.

I was taught that it was important to bring prayer flags and prayer ties to every sweat lodge ceremony I attended. I was also told to always bring offerings every full moon when the spirits are at their strongest, as well as on the new moon when the spirits are at their weakest and require our help the most. On the full moon we can pray for the things we need, while the new moon is when we thank the spirits for the things they have provided. We also make offerings and pray for the spirits to regain their strength so they can be there to help our people again in the future.

I always try to bring a food offering to every full and new moon ceremony. Along with the tobacco and cloth that are in my prayer ties, I am able to help them for another cycle of the moon. I also bring any of my hair that I have gathered over the last month. I was always told to gather it and never throw it away. I was told it was my duty to burn this as well, because our hair is considered sacred. That is why we are always being told never to let another person touch our hair, especially when it is braided.

Early picture from Marieval Indian School showing some of our local men who are all Elders in the community today or have passed on. Picture includes my Uncles Henry and Dennis.

Chapter 10

When it comes to our ceremonies, I have learned to be careful how I act and even how I think. I have been told that following certain ceremonies people become so powerful spiritually that their thoughts alone can cause bad things to happen. Because of this we are often told to stay home and remain as calm and relaxed as possible for at least four days after participating in some of these ceremonies. The spirits around you can be so strong that you cannot have any negative thoughts about anyone without causing them harm.

Some people say this is all superstition and will only hurt you if you believe in it. Personally, I have learned not to challenge the spirits by tempting fate in this way. If some people choose to call these ways nothing more than superstition or hocus pocus, that is their personal opinion, and they are entitled to that much.

However, I believe in the spirit world and have seen enough to know better than to laugh or make fun of things like this. As a parent and a grandparent, I choose not to do anything that can come back and hurt these people the Creator has blessed me with. This is why I try my very best to respect the teachings every day.

One of the first things that First Nations Elders teach is that everything we do in life comes with a consequence. Nothing is ever free, and in the end, there is always a price someone has to pay. When you play with medicines and spirituality to get ahead, it always comes back on you or your family. This means that when you take something you must always be prepared to give something back or have it taken from you by the grandfathers.

I know someone in Saskatchewan who went to a Sundance in Manitoba and was told to give away all his dance regalia before leaving the ceremonial grounds. Instead of giving it away, he traded his star blanket to a lady for a nice pair of beaded moosehide moccasins. When he arrived home, everyone told him that what he did was wrong and that he should give the moccasins to an Elder and explain what he had done. Instead, he chose to keep them and sat down to try them on. Within a week he developed a bad infection on the bottom of his foot and ended up having it amputated a few weeks later. Whether that was just coincidence or not is up to you to decide.

I have also seen people attempting to make pipes without being given the right to do so. I was always told that if you have not earned that right, you should not even be touching the sacred pipestone. Pipes are considered sacred items for a reason, and each one has its own spirit. Playing with this can have serious side effects that can not only affect you, but your loved ones as well.

The people doing this do not seem to understand that a pipe has a spirit that requires a certain ceremony to awaken it. Unless this ceremony has been performed by a qualified person, no one should touch the pipe or attempt to use it. That is why many of these pipes simply explode or fall apart when someone tries to fill them. This is another prime example of why Elders have said it is necessary to make sure of who the person is you are working with, because what they are doing can hurt you and anyone around you.

This same teaching applies to the sweat lodge. People think they can just put up a lodge and start conducting ceremonies without earning the right to do so. I have seen people who did not know better end up being hurt in many ways. Look at the recent story from the United States that was on CNN involving a non-Aboriginal man who ran what he was proclaiming to be a spiritual retreat.

James Arthur Ray, who was described in the news story as a motivational speaker and a world-renowned author, began offering what he called a "new life" to anyone willing to put their life in his hands. Because he knew how to speak to people and how to make himself sound convincing, all the people listened to him and willingly went along with whatever he asked them to do. This is something our Aboriginal Elders will tell you is foolish, and you should walk away from it.

A group consisting of fifty-six people from all walks of life paid over one thousand dollars each to take part in what this man James Arthur Ray was describing as a "Spiritual Warriors Retreat" being held in Sedona, Arizona. This is something that he claims to have done many times in the past without any problems.

During this retreat he informed everyone they would have to take part in what he described as an "American Indian sweat lodge." This, he informed everyone, would consist of eight rounds, each lasting fifteen to twenty minutes. Most First Nations sweat lodge ceremonies will only consist of four rounds or fewer, depending on the type of ceremony being conducted.

Normally, each of the rounds will acknowledge one of the four sacred directions and will not have time limits for when you can call for the door to be opened. This is up to each person attending the lodge. If for whatever reason you are unable to carry on, you simply call out, "All my relations," and the door is opened for you to leave.

However, prior to entering this so-called sweat lodge, everyone was required to participate in a thirty-six-hour fast, which left most of the members weak and tired. Despite some of the people getting sick and losing consciousness as early as the second round, James Ray refused to stop and allow anyone to leave. He kept telling everyone they were stronger than this, and if they really and truly wanted this new life he had promised to them, they all needed to wait for the end of the ceremony before they could leave.

Of the fifty-six people who took part in James Arthur Ray's so-called retreat, twenty-one ended up being rushed to the hospital in critical condition. Two people were pronounced dead at the scene, and another ended up in a coma and died nine days later. While all of this was happening around him, James Ray simply walked away from the lodge and made no attempt to help the participants—some of whom were near death.

James Arthur Ray was eventually charged in connection with the three deaths and found guilty of negligent homicide. However, in the end he only received two years in jail for his costly actions—less than one year for each victim.

This man was not even First Nations, and yet people were willing to pay him thousands of dollars to attend what he was claiming to be an Indian ceremony. No one taught this man how to do these things, he just decided to imitate something he seen somewhere else, and this was the devastating result of his foolish actions. None of the people who luckily managed to survive this ordeal will ever be the same again. Some will have to go through life with various levels of permanent brain damage as a result of this man's foolish actions.

This is why I make a point of telling people to take their time and carefully choose the people they willingly follow into any ceremony. Always remember that true Elders do not charge fees for conducting spiritual retreats or sweat lodge ceremonies. They do it because it is their responsibility to take care of the people.

I have also seen some of our own people hurt by their actions in the sweat lodge. One man I had sweated with for a long time left for a visit to Manitoba and was invited to take part in some of their ceremonies. When he returned a few months later he began claiming the spirit of a grandmother was entering him during the second round of the ceremony. This is the section they referred to as the "grandmother round." He claimed this spirit was using him to speak to the people in attendance.

During the ceremony, this man would start talking in what he pretended was the voice of an old woman. This was apparently something he had witnessed while attending one of the ceremonies in Manitoba, and now he was trying to imitate what he had seen. Many people told him he should stop doing it, but he refused to listen. One day he was unable to get himself out of bed without holding on to something, and he had to have help walking.

Within the next few weeks his condition became worse and the many doctors and specialists that he went to could not find anything wrong with him. When I last saw him, he was walking bent over with people on either side to aid him. Someone made the comment that now he was being forced to walk just like an old woman. It was heartbreaking to see him like this because he was one of the most active people I knew before all this happened.

Over the last few years, his family has taken him to all sorts of ceremonies in an attempt to help him, but nothing they tried was able to change his condition. I asked one of my most respected Elders back home if there was anything that could be done in a case like this. I was told yes, but the person involved would have to make amends to the spirit that he offended. This is not as easy as it sounds.

The spirits might even require him to put down the pipe bundle that was passed on to him and stop running sweat lodge ceremonies. Sometimes this is the price that we as human beings have to accept and learn to live with. This man was a big-house Spirit Dancer long before he decided to pick up the pipe bundle and practise sweat lodge. He was told by more than one Elder that it was time for him to do the right thing and put down that pipe so he could return to his own teachings from the big house.

Sometimes when things like this happen there are people out there who claim it is a result of someone using what they refer to as "bad medicine" on the person. When I hear people making this claim, I tell them there is really no such thing as bad medicine, there are only bad people. Medicines can be used for either good or bad. This is what I have been taught by every Elder I have worked with.

This is also the reason I am so careful whose medicines I use or touch. If I do not know where the medicines came from or who picked them, I do not like to touch them at all. Sometimes this offends people, but I have to do as I was taught and protect myself at all times. When medicines are not picked in a proper manner by people who are in the right frame of mind, these medicines are useless.

When someone goes out to pick medicines, he or she must maintain a spiritual mind frame at all times. This means they must be continuously praying and putting tobacco down as they are picking the medicines. If they are just laughing and telling stories about their past lives and how they used to drink and carry on, then this is the energy these medicines will carry. They will have no positive energy at all, only the negative energy that the people picking it carried.

Although I have absolutely no doubts that a spirit can enter someone's body and communicate through them, it is not safe to pretend to have this ability if you do not. You could end up offending the spirits, as well as the people who are sitting in the lodge with you at the time. Whenever this type of situation occurs and I feel that whatever is happening is not real, I will call for the door and leave the lodge immediately. At times like this you have to trust in your judgement. Do not second guess yourself; always trust that little voice trying to warn you.

The Creator has given us these things to use in a good way, but sadly there are always those individuals who think they can use these medicines and ceremonies for their own benefit and gain. This usually works for a while, but in the end, everyone has to pay for the things they do. I was always told it falls back on your loved ones first, and it eventually works its way down to you. Nothing comes without cost. Sometimes it comes back on you in the way of sickness or loss of the things you care about the most in life, which usually means your loved ones. If these people mean anything to you, do not play around with these sacred practices.

We always have to remember these spirits are not only very real, but they are not all alike. Some of them can be extremely powerful and are not meant to be abused or challenged in any way. If you ask someone who believes in the Spirit World, they will tell you these ancestors should be treated with absolute respect or left alone. They are capable of hurting people.

Only those who are qualified to call upon these spirits should be conducting these ceremonies. They are the only ones who should be attempting to speak with them or interpreting their messages. Someone who does not know what they are doing could misinterpret the message the spirits are sending and end up unintentionally hurting someone they are trying to help.

Over the past thirty years I have taken part in a number of Vision Quest ceremonies, as well as what is referred to as "Shaking Tent ceremonies." These are two of the types of ceremonies not recommended for people who are new to the Red Road or easily frightened by things they do not understand. I have seen many people leave these ceremonies traumatized by the events that took place.

When attending these ceremonies, the spirits sometimes show you things that can startle and even terrify you. I always tell people to speak to someone who is knowledgeable in that type of ceremony before choosing to attend one, so you will know the protocols and will not unknowingly offend anyone—especially anyone from the Spirit World.

I was told that when you decide to participate in a ceremony, you must go into it with a clean and clear mind. While in the ceremony, always be aware of your thoughts and try not to allow your mind to wander aimlessly or entertain foolish thoughts. When the person conducting the ceremony asks if you have any questions, then and only then should you allow your line of thought to revert to your questions. Still, you must be careful what you ask because you might not like the answer.

You must always remember that the spirits can understand what you are thinking, and often take things literally, so you have to be careful what you think. One Elder told me the spirits often know what you are going to ask before you get the words out, so keep your thoughts pure.

Over the years I have been told by numerous Elders from all over the country that I should never ask to see these spirits, or even foolishly wonder what they look like. I was told that a young man who was attending a Shaking Tent ceremony once asked the spirit to show himself, and when it did the man became so frightened that his hair instantly went from dark to white. The Elder told us the young man never spoke another word after leaving the ceremony. This happened over twenty years ago; the man is now in his fifties and rarely leaves his house.

Again, some people say these things only work if you believe in them, but I know that is not true. A Métis man I know well was working for Correctional Service Canada (CSC) and decided he wanted to attend a Shaking Tent in Saskatchewan, just to see what the fuss was about. He said his job required him to work closely with Aboriginal offenders and he saw that Native spirituality was now becoming a big thing within CSC. He thought that being a strong Christian would protect him from any kind of spirit that might come his way during the ceremony.

He said he was just sitting in the dark during the ceremony, listening quietly, when he thought he saw a light shine in his face. When he opened his eyes, he saw an eagle perched in front of him. He told me he felt as though he could reach out and touch it. Although the room was absolutely dark, he could see the eagle as though they were outside. He said he could even feel a cool breeze on his face from its wings as it stretched and flapped them. As it began to blink, he said its eyes looked so lifelike he was amazed by the vision before him.

He said he could still hear the person conducting the ceremony, as well as the people singing. As he continued to stare at the eagle in amazement and listen to its loud chirping sounds, he began to think that this had to be nothing more than some sort of crazy hallucination caused by the medicines being used in the ceremonial smudge.

He no sooner had the thought than the eagle turned its head and gazed directly at him. Before he realized what was happening, it began to speak to him. He said that the eagle even called him by his name before admonishing him for his behaviour at work. The eagle apparently told him it did not like the way he was treating its people and warned him to change his ways. The eagle told him there was a lot of responsibility being placed upon his shoulders, but he had the ability to help his people in a good way and this is what he should be doing, instead of holding them back.

The following morning when he arrived at work, he was afraid to tell his fellow staff members what he had seen for fear of being ridiculed or labelled crazy. After we convinced him to talk with the Elders about what he had seen he felt much better. Before leaving that day, he told everyone that he may have been a doubter when he went into the ceremony, but he was now a believer in Native spirituality, and he would take a lot more pride in his own Métis culture.

When I try to tell people about some of the things I have witnessed over the years, things that happened to individuals who chose to play around with these ceremonies, they think it is all coincidental. Most of these people have been brainwashed by society or the churches into believing there is no truth behind the stories. They equate our stories to the old devil worship campaign they have been promoting for years.

Nothing I say will convince them that the grandfathers may become offended by something the individual was saying or doing at the time. These people are simply unable to accept that the spirits are real and capable of doing things to anyone who angers or offends them.

I have witnessed people try to make a pipe even though they have not earned the right to carry one. Sometimes they will work at it for weeks only to have the pipe explode or fall apart on them the first time they try to use it. They do not understand the pipe has a spirit of its own that needs to be awakened in the proper manner. When I tell them there is a specific ceremony that must be carried out before they can use the pipe, they have no idea what I am talking about. They know nothing about the protocol that must be followed.

Most people do not know the story behind the pipestone that is used, or the significance of the different parts of the pipe. This is why we are told never to play around with things we do not understand. We stand the risk of hurting ourselves, as well as the people we love and care about the most. Just like the story of the White Buffalo Calf Pipe states, not everyone is allowed to handle the pipe, and some will not even see it. There is a reason for all of this: some people do not have the respect or humility necessary to handle such sacred objects. When people follow the Black Road, they become so contaminated they must go through numerous cleansing ceremonies before they are considered clean enough to handle, or even be in the presence of, such objects.

I first came into contact with the pipe when I was a young man visiting with family members on my home reserve. My younger brother and I were walking through the bushes near an old house that once belonged to a distant relative. As we walked along a trail that was often used as a cut-across to get to the main road heading toward the band office, we spotted something lying next to a large tree. When I picked it up, we realized it was the bowl of a red pipe. Not knowing any better at the time, I put it in my jacket pocket and proceeded on to my mother's house.

A few days later I showed it to my grandmother, who gave me a severe scolding. She asked if I could remember where we found it and told me to leave a tobacco offering on the very spot. She told me I should never pick things like this up, because we do not know who carried it or why they left it out there. When I went back to the tree, I found the wooden stem leaning up against it. I felt astonished—I know it was not there when we found the pipe bowl the week before.

When I took the pipe to an Elder who lived on one of the nearby reserves, he laughed and told me the pipe had chosen me, so it was up to me to learn how to take proper care of it. After spending time with the Elder, we determined I was not yet ready for such a responsibility. The Elder told me to wrap the pipe in sage after smudging it and place it in a bundle he provided to me. He told me to place it in a spot he chose for me. "Come back when you are ready to learn," was the last thing he said to me, and I was off to the city once again.

Choosing to walk away from that pipe and return to my old lifestyle of partying and hanging out with the same crowd of troubled friends was not the smartest thing I could have done that day. From that day forward my life began to spiral out of control, and before long I found myself in and out of jail.

When I was in residential school, people repeatedly told me the only thing I had to look forward to was being a drunk, like everyone else on the reserve, so I decided to prove them right and be the biggest drunk they had ever seen. They told me I would be useless and lazy, so I showed them they were not wrong. I did not care anymore. The more society tried to correct me, the harder I fought back and dug my heels in. I was going to show them all I could be just as stubborn as them.

The growing monument outside of the old Kamloops Indian residential school shows the depth to which this tragedy has touched people. More than just First Nations people are making their way to Kamloops to pay their respects and leave small offerings.

Chapter 11

Despite the number of years, I have spent dealing with the racism and abuse I experienced as a child, I still find it extremely difficult to talk to most non-Native people about aspects of our cultural and spiritual beliefs. I suppose it boils down to the fact I am afraid of being called crazy or stupid for believing in such things when the rest of society considers it all to be nothing more than nonsense.

When I was still young, I would often sit and listen to groups of local non-Native people talking in the coffee shop. They were always condemning our Elders for talking about things like the little people or the Spirit World. Because of this attitude toward our beliefs, I have always refused to speak openly about the experiences I have gone through over the years, even around people I knew well.

For instance, back when I was twelve and still attending the residential school in Lebret, I had a close friend named Greg who asked me one day to go for a walk, claiming he had something important to tell me. Not knowing what to expect, I agreed, and we walked to an old bridge near the lake on the edge of the school property. This was one of my favourite places to go whenever I needed to get away from everything and spend quiet time alone with my thoughts.

As we walked across the exercise yard, he told me there were things that were bothering him at night. My first thought was that the dreadful night-watchman incident from my first school was happening all over again. However, as I listened intently, I realized it was not only different, but it was something I could not have imagined in my wildest dreams. I was in shock and did not know what to think or say.

Greg began explaining how he would often be woken up at night by strange noises and something pulling hard on his blankets. This, he claimed, was happening once or twice a week. He told me that he opened his eyes one night to see what he described as a little man of less than two feet tall trying to climb onto his bed with him. It was using the blankets, which had slid off the bed and were now low enough to reach the floor.

When the little man saw he was awake, he quickly scurried away, racing under the long row of beds containing the other sleeping boys. Greg said that he could hear him laughing in a childlike tone.

Greg told me that when it first happened, he thought he was only dreaming and went immediately back to sleep. However, after the second and third time he began to get scared, but he quickly realized these little people were not trying to harm anyone. Greg said that as they slowly got to know and trust in him, they began to get bolder with each visit, sometimes even standing alongside him on the edge of his bed as he lay there watching them.

After a few months they began to show up almost nightly, and there were usually two or three of them together, he explained excitedly. He could hear their laughter and see their small arms waving back and forth as they spoke to one another, but it was impossible to make out exactly what they were talking about because they sounded like the chipmunks on the Saturday-morning cartoons. They simply spoke too fast for anyone to understand what they were trying to say, and the language they were speaking did not sound familiar.

I never knew Greg to lie or make things up. He just was not that kind of person, so I believed everything he was telling me. Although I had never seen any of these little people with my own eyes, I was always careful not to say anything that might offend them in any way. I often wondered how I would react if they suddenly chose to appear to me.

I knew that these little people existed, because when I was still a small child living at home on the reservation I would often sit quietly off to the side and listen to the older people talking amongst themselves. I would find it fascinating when they began talking about the Spirit World or those little people, who were always seen by the Elders as powerful entities.

As I grew up, I heard all sorts of stories from the many adults who came to visit. One such story claimed these little people lived in one of the ravines along the reserve, so no one ever played around that area. Even when people were out horseback riding, they would make an effort to detour around that particular area of the valley. People would often say if you went out there on calm nights and stood very still on the open prairie, just above the ravine, you could hear their singing as it echoed through the valley.

One of the local Elders said that people only went there to leave medicines, or to make offerings of cloth and tobacco when they were asking for prayer. This brought back memories about going out there with one of my older relatives and seeing prayer ties and cloth flags tied to the trees all along that section of the ravine. There was also what appeared to be a small altar made of earth with plates of food sitting on it. Obviously, someone had recently stopped by and made these offerings. I was told these little people liked sweets, so we would always offer peppermint candies to them. When we had no candies, we would leave sugar cubes, which was something I saw my grandmother do when I visited her home. She told me that as long as you gave them offerings of sweets or sugar cubes, they would not play tricks on us or hide things. She told me these little people like to hide things on you, and that sometimes when she is cleaning, she would find piles of missing things, especially if they were shiny. This was why my grandmother always had a small saucer with sweets sitting under her big wood stove in the main kitchen of her old house.

When Greg first told me about his encounters with the little people, I told him what my grandmother and the Elders from back home had told me. We began leaving a small saucer under his bed full of peppermint candies from the school canteen. Because of where his bed was, we could easily push the saucer up into the corner where none of the other boys could see it. Every evening before the rest of the boys began preparing for bed, we would quietly go up to the dormitory area and check on the saucer. It was always empty, so we would refill it.

We carried on with this nightly ritual for the next few years until I left in December of 1971 at the age of sixteen. A few years later, when I was visiting with family on the reserve, I ran into Greg and asked him about his little people. He smiled and said they were still visiting him regularly. Apparently, they had followed him home from the school. He said that once they choose you, they will never leave you unless you ask them to.

As we visited, he told me that nowadays he just refers to them as his "little helpers." I just accepted what he said and never bothered to ask him why. This would all be made clear to me years later when I first began my Healing Journey in 1989, when I started participating in some of the various ceremonies I had been introduced to while I was incarcerated.

In 1996, while participating in one of my Vision Quest ceremonies in Saskatchewan with a Grandmother Elder named Rita Parenteau from the Wahpeton Dakota First Nation and another visiting Elder from the Pine Ridge area in South Dakota, I finally got to see these little people for myself. At first, I did not realize what I had seen in my vision. Only after one of my Elders pointed out details from the Vision Quest was I able to realize what I had been shown in the ceremony.

On the third day of the Vision Quest ceremony, I found myself following what appeared to be a well-worn path through some thick brush. I slowly walked along the path, listening to the birds singing their different songs and doing my best to enjoy the beautiful scenery. Before long, I arrived at a clearing and noticed two men dressed in buckskin sitting beside a small fire. They were trying to pull apart what appeared to be a large ceremonial pipe. I decided to stop and watch them for a while.

One of the men held on firmly to the extra-large stem with both hands while the other held tightly to the huge bowl. The man holding the bowl began pulling hard and turning it at the same time. I could hear loud screeching sounds as the stem was twisted back and forth inside the bowl, but it would not come apart no matter how hard the two men twisted and pulled. It appeared to be an impossible task, but they would not give up.

The men appeared oblivious to my presence as they continued to struggle patiently with the task before them. They laughed loudly and shook their heads before turning the pipe around so the other man could have a turn pulling and twisting the stem. I noticed that the pipe's bowl was red on one side and black on the other, almost like it was made up of two different pipe halves that were somehow stuck together, something I had never seen before.

No matter what the two men did, they just could not seem to accomplish anything. When they finally set the pipe down to take a break, I decided to carry on with my journey and quietly proceeded down the path once again. As I left and continued on my way, I could hear them talking in a language I had never heard before. I found it odd that I could see and hear them, but they paid no notice to me or the fact I was leaving without a word. It was almost like the two men could not see me standing there watching them. Was I somehow in spirit form, I wondered?

When the Vision Quest ceremony was over and I had time to sit and talk with my Elders about what I had seen, they both laughed and told me to take a few more days to meditate about everything. The Elders knew I was not focusing on the big picture, so they wanted me to slow down my mind and rethink everything I had been shown. I was far too busy focusing my thoughts on the pipe of two colours to take notice of anything else I had seen. They kept telling me to close my eyes and revisit everything.

When we gathered for our weekly sweat lodge ceremony three days later, the Elders decided to let me off the hook. Merle Whistler, the Elder from South Dakota, asked me to explain to them why I thought the pipe in my vision was large. After laughing for a while, he told me I needed to consider the possibility that the pipe was the correct size, and it was the two people who were small. When he said this, I was flabbergasted. You could have knocked me over with a feather. Only after he said all of this did it all begin to make sense, and I felt foolish about the whole thing.

How could I have not seen any of this for myself? I had always been taught not to be quick to jump to conclusions and to always make sure I saw the big picture. I had clearly not done any of this. The men both wore beaded buckskins and moccasins, just like regular people, so I could not tell that anything was different from the clothing. Still, how could I not see any of this on my own? I had been working closely with so many different Elders that it was a shock to me to not be able to see the big picture at a time like this.

Maybe this was just the grandfathers' way of telling me that I still have a long way to go, and I do not know as much as I like to think I do. This was clearly their way of reminding me that I am human, and rather than thinking I have been taught everything I must learn how to be humbler. I must learn to slow down and be more aware of my surroundings. One of my Elders told me to always expect the unexpected and I would never miss anything. This is a piece of advice I do not plan on forgetting.

When we were about to leave the ceremony, both of my Elders told me that these little people were now my spirit helpers. I was told not to be afraid to ask them for help when I was praying for someone or something. I was also told that the little people are considered very special helpers, and that I should consider myself incredibly lucky because they chose me. When they told me this I felt much better about the whole thing, and I immediately put some candy on the mound in front of our lodge and said a prayer for my friend Greg and his little helpers. Somehow, I just cannot help feeling that he is responsible for introduced me to *my* little helpers.

Prior to this Vision Quest I had already been given two other spirit helpers. The first was the mountain lion, or *Ihumu Tanka* in the Sioux language. This helper came with my Dakota name Ta'wacine O'hitika, which means, "The One with the Strong/Brave Mind." The second helper I was given was a frog that came to me in a separate Vision Quest ceremony a few years earlier. I was told it was a healer, and this meant I now had three spirit helpers to call upon whenever I needed help or guidance of any kind.

Another terrible experience I had was after attending a sweat lodge ceremony in British Columbia. During the ceremony we all experienced the Elder's eagle fan and buffalo rattle flying around inside the lodge while he prayed for everyone in attendance, along with their families. I could not only hear them as they moved around, I could feel them as they moved behind and above me. Although this was not the first time I experienced this effect, I prayed harder and thanked the Creator for the experience. This is something that has always amazed me no matter how many times I experience it.

When the sweat was over, one of the non-Native people who was with us during the ceremony began making all sorts of negative comments about the ceremony. He went so far as to accuse the Elder of resorting to trickery to try to impress everyone, and to make us believe he had supernatural powers.

Because of people like this, most First Nations people refuse to share their personal experiences, even with each other. We have been brainwashed into believing that our ways are worthless and not as important as the dominant European beliefs, most of which stem from the churches and their Christian beliefs.

Today when I sit and think about all these wonderful people, I have had the pleasure of meeting and learning from over the years, I still cannot help but wonder how different my life might have been had they been there all along, guiding me and teaching me about life, just as our ancestors have done for thousands of years. Keeping that spiritual circle strong would have surely kept me on the right path and helped to ensure that I became the kind of person that I now struggle so hard to find within myself.

In the years after leaving residential school, I struggled with alcohol and drug abuse. This lifestyle led me in and out of jail for a number of years, beginning when I turned nineteen. Although I am not proud of this time in my life, I have to acknowledge that going to jail probably saved my life. This was where I finally found the support to get back to my cultural and spiritual teachings. Sadly, this is also the harsh truth for most First Nations men who have found their way back to the Red Road.

Considering the direction that my life was heading before my return to the Red Road, I would more than likely have died of a drug overdose, or an alcohol-related incident. Over the past thirty years I have seen most of my old acquaintances from that previous lifestyle all slowly succumb to some form of substance-related death. Most of them were dead before their fortieth birthdays, even some of the people from my home community who I grew up with who were all much younger than me.

Today I am a sixty-four-year-old man and, sadly, I have to admit I have spent more than half my life in prison. When I visit any First Nation community, I find this is true for most of the men my age. I suppose we were all running from the same demons that have been haunting most residential school survivors for years. I can only hope and pray that more of these survivors will find their way back to the Red Road or get whatever help they so desperately need to begin their own Healing Journeys. We must begin focusing on this not just for ourselves, but for the next seven generations that will follow in our footsteps.

Chasing that self-destructive lifestyle of drugs and alcohol has taken us away from our loved ones and caused nothing but sadness and pain in our communities. It has become the prime cause of most family violence and breakups within First Nations communities. It is also the main reason for most of our First Nations men and women ending up in the overcrowded correctional system. We have to start understanding that these substances were never a part of our culture. These things were brought here by the colonizers and have been used to destroy our people.

When I think back, I admit that a lot of the things that sent me in and out of those correctional facilities were just plain stupid. I can remember being released at 7:00 a.m. from the old Regina Correctional Centre only to find myself sitting back in the city cells by suppertime waiting to see the judge in the morning. I was walking from one bar to another, and apparently, I got tired, because I decided to help myself to someone else's car even though the bar I was heading to was only three blocks away.

This was how crazy my life had become. I did not seem to care what the world did to me anymore. It seemed as though I had decided to become every negative thing I had been called since I was a child. People told me that the only thing I had to look forward to was being a drunk like everyone else on the reserve, so I unwittingly decided to prove them all right. They told me that I was useless and lazy, so once again I decided to prove them right.

For years I found it extremely difficult to understand why my life was so out of control. During one of my many periods of incarceration, I was introduced to a young Native court worker who explained to me what it meant to be institutionalized. This was not something I was eager to accept. I spent the next few years trying hard to convince myself that this could not possibly be true.

I even told myself this was just the federal government's latest way of deciding what was best for me.

However, the words that the young court worker said to me must have carried some truth, because they stayed with me for years. It was not until ten years later after numerous stays in halfway houses and rehab centres that I finally began to take notice that some of the things he said had some truth to them. With this sudden realization I was not only forced to look at myself in a new light, but I was also forced to re-evaluate everything I had come to believe about myself. Once again it brought up the old question: Are we really who we think we are, or are we who people tell us we are?

The most obvious thing I had noticed was that as long as I was living in one of these facilities, I did great. I even managed to stay clean and sober as long as I had the structure and supervision that the facility provided. When I was eventually released with a few dollars in my pocket, I would find myself almost immediately drawn back to the lifestyle that ended with me right back in jail. It was a never-ending cycle that I was now beginning to recognize and hate.

The last time I was in one of these federal institutions, I met an Elder from the Little Shuswap area. His name was Ernie Phillips, and he was in his early seventies. He had come to the institution to demonstrate his talents as a Pow-wow dancer. This was something he was quite good at, after years of practice.

When we stopped for a lunch break, he came over and sat down with our drum troupe and began talking about culture and spirituality. I explained to him how an awful lot of the First Nations men inside these institutions, myself included, were afraid of getting back out into the real world. Most of them waive their parole dates and are more than willing to sit in the institution and continue doing time until the end of their sentence arrives. Only then will they reluctantly walk out the front doors and return to the community and the family they left behind.

Ernie told us that when you leave a place like prison it can become a difficult struggle to regain your spirit. He always tells the young men and women he meets at these events that when their time comes to move on, they must be prepared spiritually, or they will come right back. He told us that we must begin by calling our spirit. This means you must call out your Indian name four times as you are leaving and never look back behind you, no matter what.

If you do not have an Indian name, he said to call out the name that your parents gave you at birth. This is because you do not want to leave any part of your spirit behind, or you will be drawn back by it. When you are doing this, he told us, you are showing your ancestors on the other side that you do not care for this place and that you want no part of it ever again.

Ernie pointed out the sad fact that most of the men are residential school survivors who are too comfortable in the prison setting. They are not only institutionalized but they have gotten used to their daily routines and do not care to change anything. They are psychologically seeing this prison life as being back in their old school setting once again. This is why First Nations people often refer to the correctional system as the new residential schools.

Some of these men have established themselves inside and are afraid of losing everything if they are forced to move on. Some of them have taken on important roles within the institution, such as around the sweat lodge or within the Aboriginal Brotherhood group. Sadly, they see these roles as sufficient and are afraid that, if they get out tomorrow, they will become nobodies again.

Everything Ernie told us made sense and was no different than what all the institutional Elders have been trying to teach the men and women inside. Unfortunately, they can only carry the message so far, and we as grown men have to start listening and accepting what the Elders are trying to teach us.

Chapter 12

In September of 2012, while I was still residing in the city of Kamloops, I stopped at the grocery store to pick up some lunch supplies for a trip into the mountains to gather lava rocks with a friend of mine who needed grandfathers for his lodge on the nearby reserve. While standing in the checkout line I was approached by a young man from the Kamloops Indian Band. I had met him a few weeks earlier at a Pow-wow on the Fountain First Nation near the town of Lillooet.

He knew that I loved to sing Pow-wow and that I often sat in with different groups of singers. He told me that a group of young men from his community asked him if he wanted to join them in their attempt to form a drum troupe of their own. Some of these boys were pretty good singers, so he decided to join them for a while. Like most young men out there, he assumed this would be a good way to meet girls.

After about three months he learned that two of the young men, brothers as well as the owners of the big drum they were using, were partying heavily and always kept the drum in their SUV along with the alcohol and drugs. When he asked them about this, they laughed at him and told him not to be so old-fashioned. Then they began teasing him about being superstitious and told him he should not place so much emphasis on any of those old stories, as they were clearly just meant to scare children.

A few days later they gathered to practice singing, and one of the brothers began teasing him again, asking if he was too scared to sing with them now. As they sat there laughing, they heard a loud cracking noise and what sounded like something snapping. They looked around, trying to figure out what had caused the sudden noise. When they began to play, they realized the noise had come from the drum, which had literally caved in on one side.

The young man told me that his friends were now scared and did not know what to do with the broken drum. They were all afraid they had done something that would cause them to have bad luck. I told him not to worry, because this was just the sort of fear that comes from not knowing the proper protocol most First Nation communities attach to a ceremonial object such as a drum. I told him they should have just gone to one of their own community Elders and explained what had happened.

I told them to bring the drum to my place. They did, and we took it into the bush outside of town, along with some tobacco and cloth offerings. I explained to them this was the way I was taught by my Elders back home. After we said a prayer and they talked to the spirit of the drum, asking for its forgiveness surrounding any of the mistakes they may have made, we hung the big drum from a large branch along with the offerings they had brought and went home.

Surprisingly, when I arrived at the sweat lodge later that week for our regular ceremony, the young men were there waiting. They explained that they had taken my advice and approached one of their own community Elders, who told them to go to the sweat lodge and pray. He told them to thank the Creator and the spirit of the drum for the valuable teachings they had received from the entire event. Before going into the lodge, I told them how my Elder always told me to leave everything in there with the grandfathers and they would take care of it. Over the next few months, I would frequently run into the young men while I was in town. One day I asked them if they had tried to find another drum for themselves, and the answer they gave me was surprising. They said they had talked about it and decided they were not ready yet. I knew exactly what they were feeling, because I made all the same mistakes when I was young. As I walked away, I could not help feeling proud of the young men, because they were obviously quick learners who I am sure will be singing again before too long. The important thing is that they learn from their mistakes.

Another situation involving youth happened a few years earlier when I was attending a winter gathering in one of the many long houses situated throughout the Lower Mainland. While there I ran into a man I had not seen since the late seventies. His name was Leonard George, and he was the son of the late and well-known Native actor Chief Dan George. He told me how happy he was to see that more and more young people are finding their way back to the spiritual and cultural teachings of our ancestors.

He explained that he could see just by observing these young people which ones were taking things seriously and which ones still had not put their heart into it. These were the ones who were just there to please their family members and had not committed themselves yet. Sometimes, he said, it takes a couple of years for them to open their eyes, but at least they are here and that is what counts in the long run.

When I asked him what he meant, he told me he always watches the behaviours of the young people to see how they do things, even simple ones like whether they take care of the Elders seated around them by simply asking if they need anything when they grab a coffee for themselves. These types of actions show signs of respect and good, strong teachings.

He told me that an Elder in Saskatchewan once told him to watch one particular young man at a Round Dance gathering. When the young man opened a pack of cigarettes, he always offered the first one to the Elders seated next to him, even though none of them had come to the gathering with him. When the food was brought out later that evening, the young man served the Elders around him before getting anything for himself.

The Elder observing all of this said it was the little things like this that told him more about a person than any number of words. The Elder told Leonard that if he looked around, he would see that they were not the only ones who took notice of the young man. There were several other Elders watching as well.

The Elder went on to say that at some point in the future they were going to be looking for young people to assist as helpers in these ceremonies, and this is when the Elders will remember the young man's respectful behaviour. The Elder told Leonard that back home in British Columbia, this young man would likely be the one chosen to become a helper and future leader in the big house.

I explained to Leonard how I considered myself new to most of these teachings, and I sometimes wondered why I had allowed my life to get so out of control. I told him I sometimes felt ashamed for not knowing even the most basic teachings and protocol when I was growing up. He smiled and told me I had to learn to be patient with myself and stop trying so hard. He told me that when you are meant to know things, the Creator will find a way of showing you what you need.

Leonard explained how we as human beings have a positive and negative side. If we allow the negative side to overpower us, we end up crashing down. This is why some people fly into uncontrollable fits of rage and cannot seem to stop. This continues until they find that balance.

Everything in the universe, he told me, not only have spirits, but they have male and female sides. Everything has an opposite: one cannot exist without the other. There cannot be good without bad, happy without sad, old without new, and so on.

Leonard said these were teachings passed down to First Nations children from the time they are considered old enough to understand. He explained how the Europeans tried for so long to stop these teachings, only to see them come back stronger than ever. This is all thanks to the awakening the Elders said was coming. Even non-Natives are starting to take an interest in what our people have to say. Just look around when you are at any of the gatherings in your communities.

He is right about the culture being stronger than it has been in hundreds of years. This is because all the younger people want to show pride in who they are as a Nation. I can only hope that the next seven generations remain strong and committed to these teachings of their ancestors. This way the teachings will never die, and only get stronger.

Before saying goodbye, I asked Leonard about the importance of recognizing and acknowledging the spirits. He told me that, to all the big house people on the West Coast, this was considered particularly important. This is why they are called "Spirit Dancers." Each one has his or her own song and dance they must perform every year for the rest of their lives, and if they do not, they risk getting sick.

He told me that some people believe the spirits only come out at night, or immediately after sundown. Others believe the spirits are strongest just before dawn. The truth is that the spirits are always there. They walk amongst us at all times and are even there when we are sleeping. This is why some spirits come to visit us in our dreams and we wake up thinking it was so real. Elders will often tell us we need to pay closer attention to these dreams, because there is sometimes a message within them.

When I first began my Healing Journey back in 1989, I was afraid to talk about things like spirits or the Spirit World. Today, I realize this was because of my residential school upbringing. Back then, any such talk would result in a vicious attack by one of the Catholic nuns, who would often wash our mouths out with soap.

Today, I am intrigued by conversations surrounding spirits or the Spirit World. One of the first serious talks I took part in was a result of a young First Nations man who hanged himself while in custody at the Stony Mountain Institution in Manitoba.

Someone told the Elder in our group that he was brought up to believe that even First Nations people have a hard time crossing over if they took their own life. This resulted in one of the longest and most heated discussions our small group ever had.

The Elder told us he had heard something similar at some point in his life, but he never gave it much thought. He said he remembered hearing his grandmother speaking at a wake for someone who had taken their own life. She told the deceased person's spirit that what they had done was extremely selfish, because of all the people they had hurt by committing this act. She told the spirit that the people they had left behind would now have to pray harder than ever for the next four days and nights to ensure the spirit made its journey unimpeded.

The Elder told everyone that this was the main reason we always ask for a sweat or some other form of ceremony within four days of someone passing. This helps to ensure they have someone there to meet them and guide them to the other side peacefully. This also explains why we are always told to feed our ancestors as often as we can. That way when it is our turn to cross over, they will be there to greet us and help us get to the Spirit World in a good way.

He told us about the old superstition that people often pass in groups of three, meaning that when one dies there will usually be two more passing within the next few days. Surprisingly, a lot of First Nations people strongly believe in this. When I was growing up in the prairies, I often heard people talking about this.

The Elder was taught that this sometimes happens when someone dies suddenly and they do not understand, or they refuse to believe what is happening to them. Other times they simply become afraid and react in the only way they can. They cannot accept what is happening, so they reach out to someone they knew in life, and by doing this they force that individual to accompany them on their final journey.

I asked the Elder what happens if someone dies from a drug overdose. Would the person even know what was happening to them? Could their spirit simply continue wandering around thinking that it was just on a bad high? The Elder said he liked my question, but he had no idea what to tell me. He told me he was going to bring it up to the Sundance Chief at their next gathering, as he thought the question deserved an answer. Approximately one month later, the Elder told me he had talked to the Sundance Chief about my question and was told this kind of thing happens more often than we think. The Chief told him there are all kinds of spirits wandering aimlessly, because there is no one to guide them home to the other side. This, he said, is why we must always make an offering every time we are visited by someone from the Spirit World. He told me not to be afraid of them, just acknowledge that you know they are there and offer them food or tobacco. They will always remember you in a good way for this.

The Elder was brought up to believe that the spirits are more detectable in the evenings and just before sunrise. He said that it is almost as though the spirits are stronger during these hours. A lot of Elders will tell you this is the perfect time to feed the spirits and to make prayer ties as offerings. Most Elders I know get up early and do their morning prayers as soon as the sun begins to rise. They go outside again just before sundown to give thanks to the Creator for giving them another beautiful day.

When I asked one of my Elders from back home in Saskatchewan about all this, he smiled and told me this was why he always went outside just before sunrise to say his prayers and make an offering. The small clearing behind his house was the perfect spot, because he could see the Morning Star clearly from there and he was told to acknowledge it in his prayers.

When he told me this, I remembered what my Clan Mother told us about the Morning Star. She said that when you really want something, you have to get up early and go outside so that you can face the star. Then you say your prayer and make an offering to it, and it will grant you your prayer if you are sincere and pray straight from your heart.

Over the years, I have received a great many of these simple teachings from our Elders. Sometimes I wonder how I am supposed to remember everything they teach me, but when the time comes and I need to remember something, it always finds its way into my memory, even things that were told to me when I was so tired that I was afraid of falling asleep on the Elder. The Creator always finds a way of putting the right teaching in your head when you need it.

When I was attending a Healing Circle at the Mission Institution, a visiting Elder asked everyone something that will remain with me for the rest of my life. We were talking about the importance of family when he stopped the group and asked everyone to try to recall the last time, they told their mother they loved her. He pointed out that it was easy to pick up the phone and call her when we were in trouble. It was as though we could only tell her we loved her when we were sitting in jail.

The Elder told us we all needed to teach ourselves how to say "I love you" every day to the people in our lives. He told us that the Creator could call them or us home at any time, so we needed to start telling them how important they are to us before it was too late. We always wait until they are gone before we think about things like this.

This same Elder was the one who pointed out that we as men always like to tell our girlfriends how much we love them but asked if we ever really consider what that sentence means. He told us that if you ever truly loved someone in your lifetime, you would never be able to hate that person no matter what. If you ever end up hating the person, it was only lust, not love.

Whenever I tell this to people, I consider to be spiritual, they just smile and tell me the Elder who taught me this was very smart. Then they will tell me how they make it a point to tell their loved ones they love them as often as they can. Even if they are just going out to the corner store for a few minutes, they say "goodbye" and "I love you." This should not be hard to remember; after all, love is one of the Seven Sacred Teachings.

Chapter 13

Sadly, the one thing the residential school system did not prepare any of us for was the systemic racism that seems to dominate society. When we were in these schools, we were subjected to all sorts of abuse meant to degrade us as a people. Although this treatment was in fact connected to racist views about First Nations people, we as children were not able to make the connection at that time. Most of us knew deep down inside that this kind of treatment was wrong, but we had no idea that the rest of the world was just as filled with hate as those awful schools and the people who ran them.

I remember walking through a north-end suburb of Regina shortly after leaving the school in Lebret and having a small group of young non-native men chase me across the sports field. I saw them out of the corner of my eye as they walked slowly toward me. Without any warning, they began throwing rocks and calling me a "dirty Indian." All of this just because I attempted to cut through their schoolyard on my way downtown.

I did not know any of these people, some of whom were closer to being men than boys. I had never spoken to any of them before or had any kind of interaction with them, so I could not understand why they hated me so much. This bothered me for some time, and it eventually caused me to become apprehensive when dealing with the non-Native community around me, especially the younger people, who were often quite vocal. Most of the time they would begin yelling obscenities and racial slurs.

Over the years, I experienced many more of these altercations, which often ended in some form of violence. Even though I was often the one who was outnumbered and forced to defend myself, I would usually be the one taken away in handcuffs and charged with disturbing the peace, assault, or whatever the police could think up at the time. They too would often ask me foolish questions, like, "Why don't you just go home to the reserve where you belong?" This is the same attitude the RCMP exhibit today when they deal with members of the First Nations.

My early years spent growing up on the streets taught me how to accept and deal with people around me, no matter how ignorant or racist they chose to act toward me or my friends. I learned not to walk alone when I was in an area, I was not familiar with, especially if this was an area not frequented by other Native people. When I was alone, I learned that looking these people directly in the eyes and scowling defiantly often caused them to retreat, or at least rethink their actions. In most cases they would leave me alone.

By the time I had grown out of my teen years, I had pretty much seen it all. There were not many things in life that could surprise me anymore. I had learned not to place expectations on people, regardless of who they were or where they came from. Past experiences taught me that this was the only way to avoid disappointment.

I had been to nearly every major community between Vancouver, British Columbia, and Thunder Bay, Ontario. No matter where I went, I trusted no one and was always on guard for people trying to take advantage of me and my friends. Survival was the only thing that mattered, and I did not care who I had to step on to get what I needed.

When I think about it, our country really has not come all that far over the past sixty years. In my own lifetime, our people were not allowed to vote or walk into any kind of liquor outlet. This only began to change in the early sixties, just before I was taken away to residential school. Although we are now allowed to vote and enter any bar or liquor outlet we choose, there is still an overabundance of racial tension throughout the country. Just watch the nightly news.

I recall as a child listening to my grandfather and uncles talking about needing a permission slip to sell one of their cows at the local auction barn so they could pay some of the bills. This was also necessary whenever they finished with the fall harvest and needed to take the grain to the local elevator to sell.

My grandmother told me that at one time they even required a travel permit anytime they left the reserve, even if it was just to see the doctor in the nearby town where they received their mail. If they were caught without the permit, they could be arrested and charged. All these different permits were available only through the Indian Affairs agent in charge of a particular Indian Band.

Sometimes I would hear my uncles talking about travelling through some of the small farming communities across the valley from our reserve. They would describe these towns as nothing more than redneck communities. Some of them even had signs in front of their businesses that read no dogs or Indians allowed. This was in the sixties, which was not all that long ago either.

Although I have never seen things like this, I can recall the racist remarks we would get when our school played baseball or hockey in these farming communities. They would throw things at our school bus and call us a bunch of "dirty Indians," usually because we were the team they could not beat on the ballfield or the ice.

When I became old enough to enter the bar, I would often round up a group of my close friends on a Friday night and drive to these little towns just to sit in their hotel and goad the locals into a fight. This led to some lively weekends.

When I was still attending residential school, I would sometimes get the opportunity to go home with various relatives for the holidays. I always treasured these times, because most of these relatives had their own ways of teaching me the things I needed to know. Some of them would just tell me stories about my dad and how crazy he was when he returned home from the military.

One of my uncles from my mother's side of the family, Donald, told me he always had a lot of respect for my dad because he too had been in the military and knew what my dad had to deal with when he came home. He went from being one of the boys to being just another damned Indian.

He told me that during their time in the military, and especially during times of combat, everyone treated them like equals because they all had to count on each other for their survival. However, this all changed as soon as they arrived home to Canada, and no one needed them anymore. This is when they were discarded like trash and given no support to help them deal with their trauma.

My uncle told me that a lot of the non-Native soldiers liked having the Native men around, because they were skilled with a rifle. This came from growing up on the reservation and having to hunt to feed your family and relatives. He said that most Native men were natural warriors, and quickly became the go-to guys in the outfit for tracking and scouting enemy soldiers.

Despite all these men did for their country, most of them were given nothing when they returned home. Most of them had to fight for years to get the same pension and medical coverage as their non-Native associates. They did not even receive the same respect when they went to the Legion Hall like other former military men and women. Most were simply turned away at the door.

When I was in my early twenties, it was my Uncle Donald who explained to me how we get our traditional names. He told me that these names are not simply picked out of thin air, they are given to us at birth or passed on through one of the various ceremonies. Most times there is some form of significance attached to the name you are given.

When we go to an Elder who has been given the right to present these names, he or she will usually take you into the sweat lodge to pray about it. My uncle said that this process can sometimes take as long as two or three days, because it involves the spirits. He explained that when the Elder takes you into the lodge, they present you to the ancestors, letting them know you wish to carry a traditional name.

Once this has been done, they wait for one of the ancestors to come forward and claim you. This is when the spirit tells the Elder, "I will claim him and allow him to carry my name." From that day forward it is up to you to carry that name with humility and pride. You must acknowledge that ancestor every year with flags and tobacco offerings to say, *thank you for allowing me to carry your name.*

Uncle Donald also told me to keep in mind that when you say, "all my relations," you are talking about all living things, as well as all those residing in the Spirit World. He told me that you cannot say these words and then go out and disrespect Mother Earth or any of the things she provides for us each day. He told me that if I was having a bad day, all I have to say is, "All my relations."

When my Uncle Donald, who was a Vietnam veteran as well as a traditional dancer, passed away, he was buried in his traditional regalia, and the bottoms of his finely beaded moccasins were painted with red ochre. This, I was told, was done to help him on his final journey to the Spirit World and to protect him from anything that might try to impede him on his final journey.

I was sad to hear about my uncle's passing, but I will always remember the many wonderful things that he taught us over the years. I always try to keep in mind one simple thing he always said: "The quality of your life depends on the quality of people that you surround yourself with. So always try to surround yourself with positive people who will help you to make the right choices in life."

Despite all of the hardships that my uncle faced throughout his life, he was a very culturally oriented person. He loved to not only dance Pow-wow, but to spend time teaching the younger people how to dance traditional style. Whenever you traveled to a Pow-wow anywhere in the country, you could always find him giving some young dancer pointers on how to become better at their craft and how to catch the eyes of the people who were there judging the event.

My uncles took up the traditional role of teacher to the young men in our home community. According to our Elders, it was always the uncles who were responsible for passing on things like good work ethics and hunting skills. It is usually the role of one uncle in the family to be summoned if any of the young men in the family required discipline.

As I grew older, I became more aware of the traditional beliefs in the Sioux culture. Some of them seemed harsh or even foolish until I began to fully understand the reasoning behind these teachings. Once I learned this, everything made sense.

For instance, my aunt once told me that back when she was growing up, she was taught that a wife was never supposed to look her father-in-law in the eyes. In fact, she was not even permitted to speak to him directly. If she wanted to ask him a question, she had to ask her husband to ask his father the question for her. This applied even if the father was in the same room. These strict rules also applied to the husband and his mother-in-law.

This, I was told, was how things were, and no one questioned it. It was done out of respect for the in-laws. All men were expected to have absolute respect for their mother-in-law, and women were expected to have the same respect for their father-in-law. In the end it all worked out well for everyone, and since this was how it had always been, no one thought much about it.

My aunt said that when it came to sisters-in-law, it was considered okay for the men in the family to tease them, but in a respectful manner. Everyone understood that if anything happened to your brother, you became responsible for his family, particularly his children. This would go on until she found another husband to take care of them.

Today, no one remembers or follows these old traditional values that our ancestors practiced so diligently and believed in so strongly in. Sadly, our modern family beliefs and values fall far short of the more community-oriented lifestyle that our grandparents knew. Maybe if we went back to learning about some of their traditions and beliefs, we would have much stronger family bonds today.

In their day, the wellbeing of the entire community took precedence over our own personal wants and needs. Our ancestors did not live in a property-oriented society like we do. They thought about the community as one large family. Everyone was responsible for the wellbeing of their neighbours. No one in the community went without. I was often told that if one person was hungry, the whole community was hungry. This was just a metaphor because no one ever went hungry. There was always wild meat, fish, and plants available.

Even as a child I could tell how people in the community looked out for each other and made sure everyone had food to eat and wood for their fires. People would always stop by with fresh fish or ducks and geese they had just killed. Every fall, the men in our community would get together and hunt for moose, elk, or white-tailed deer, which would be distributed amongst the families who needed it, especially those households with no grown males to provide for them. I don't remember going hungry as a child.

As small children, we learned early what it meant to do our part for the community. When I was nine or ten, one of the local

Elders taught me and my younger brothers how to set up snares to catch rabbits and grouse. Every day we would return home proud of ourselves, because we would each have a dozen or so freshly killed rabbits and a grouse or two. These would be cleaned by our sisters and distributed to the local Elders, or to the single women with small children to feed.

I pulled a small wagon in the summer and a sleigh in the winter to deliver firewood or fresh water to the Elders who lived in our area of the reserve. My brother and I were proud of this, and we considered it our job, come rain or shine. My brother and I would turn it into a friendly competition to see who could collect the most firewood. None of this seemed like work to us; it was just part of our daily routine.

Most of the Elders were grateful and offer small treats to us as a thank you. Others would simply observe us without a word until we left. This did not bother us, because our grandmother told us that the Creator was watching, and he would make sure that someone was there to help us when we were old.

We were taught that our ancestors did not discriminate against people who were sick, elderly, or crippled. These individuals were taken care of by those who were stronger and healthier. This was their way of living by the Seven Sacred Teachings.

One of the oldest Elders in my home community was a man named Charlie, who was born sometime in the late 1890s. My cousin Lawrence and I would stop by his small cabin, which sat just off the road allowance along the main road into the reserve. We knew that he was considered Métis by the Canadian government, but to us he was just another Elder.

He was always happy to see visitors, no matter how old they were. He would begin by offering us a hot cup of tea before sharing stories and teachings from his childhood. He would tell us that our people were not prejudiced against anyone. The only people we did not like were those who intended harm against our community. These people were considered enemies and often dealt with harshly.

The Elder would tell us stories about people who refused to accept or live by these values, only thinking of themselves. These people would take from others and squander their time drinking and fighting amongst themselves. When the community eventually grew tired of their behaviour, they would be banished and told not to return. Their few meagre belongings would be given to relatives or divided amongst community members who they owed.

Chapter 14

Last week, I was at a memorial Pipe Ceremony for one of my favourite Elders who had recently passed on. When the feather was passed around and I had the opportunity to talk, I did my best to speak respectfully from the heart, just the way I had been taught. I spoke about the many wonderful things that I had learned from this man, and how my people dealt with the grief that comes from losing someone who is significant in our lives.

When the ceremony was over, I had one of the newer Elders in the community walk over and tell me that he was happy and somewhat surprised to see how much knowledge I had about cultural and spiritual teachings. At first, I was bothered by his off-the-cuff comment. Not that I thought he was trying to be sarcastic or facetious, I just felt uncomfortable having someone point this out. We are always told to be humble in our daily life, and I suppose I simply felt uncomfortable with someone praising me like that.

As we talked, I began to understand what he was getting at. He said that, considering where I had received most of my teachings, he thought they were stronger than those I would have received in the community. I disagreed with him, of course, but soon reminded myself that he was entitled to his own opinion.

He was referring to the fact that I was first introduced to my First Nations culture and spirituality while serving time in jail. He told me he had the opportunity to work with inmates in Manitoba, and because of this he knew how difficult it was to follow the Red Road with all the distractions and temptations surrounding incarcerated people. He said it is probably worse than living in a skid-row alley.

Inmates have to deal with violence and other negative distractions on a daily basis. Sometimes other inmates will see that you are trying to improve yourself and taunt you in an attempt to see just how far they can push you before you get angry. Then they laugh and say stupid things like, "See, I knew you were just pretending to be spiritual."

Others will try to tempt you with drugs and homemade alcohol. Luckily, I had sweat lodge brothers who watched out for one another and were quick to come running whenever a brother was in trouble. This was what kept most of the troublemakers at bay. They did not want to have to deal with forty-two angry brothers.

The Elder told me a story that came from the Sundance in South Dakota. He said that an elderly Medicine Man who was blind since birth was conducting a Pipe Ceremony for all the people about to dance. During the ceremony, he talked about a vision he had had following the previous Sundance. This vision told him about a whole new generation of dancers and pipe carriers. These men and women carried strange marks on their bodies that were not from the sacred Sundance ceremony.

The blind Medicine Man told everyone that these new pipe carriers and spiritual people would be much stronger than anyone from his generation. The strength they will possess will be because of the places they were forced to receive their spiritual teachings. With so much negative energy surrounding them, it will take great strength on their part to remain humble.

Only when the ceremony was finished, and everyone began to slowly get up and leave did someone finally figure out that the Elder was talking about brothers and sisters who are incarcerated. Those strange marks he referred to were the tattoos that most of these people now carry on their bodies. These brothers and sisters are picking up the old ways and returning to the sacred teachings in an effort to turn their lives around and begin teaching the next seven generations.

When the story was finished, I turned to the people I was sitting with and began explaining how sad I sometimes feel, because I had to admit that nearly all my teachings were passed on to me while I was in prison. This is a sad reality for most men from my generation. We lost our cultural and spiritual teachings to the years we spent confined inside of the government's awful residential school system, years that none of us will ever regain, no matter how much compensation they throw at us.

My introduction to the cultural and spiritual teachings began when I was twenty. I ended up inside the Regina Correctional Centre in 1975, serving a one-year sentence for auto theft. While there I was introduced to a visiting Elder from one of the local reserves. We did not have sweat lodges inside the walls in those days, but the Elders were allowed to come in and talk to any of us willing to learn.

This was also the first time I took part in a Pipe Ceremony. It was just over a year earlier that I had found the pipe leaning up against the tree on my home reserve, the very pipe I would later learn to respect and use whenever I was in need of spiritual help and guidance, something that would happen more times than I care to remember, but it was all part of growing up.

However, before I reached that moment in my life, I had to deal with the demons that had control over my world. For the next ten years I lived a lifestyle that led me in and out of one jail cell after another. Most of my visits to these places were because of property-related charges, meaning I would steal other people's property whenever the opportunity presented itself. This allowed me and my friends to finance our lifestyle of drugs and alcohol.

Like most young men, I did not care that I was being sent to jail for months or even years at a time. I treated it like a game, seeing how much I could get away with before they caught me. The longest I spent between sentences was just over a year. This was because my daughter Marilyn was born, and I wanted to stay home and spend time with her. She is the most special gift the Creator has put into my life.

For the first time in years, I managed to stay sober and straight. I even began doing honest work for the first time in my life. There I was, building houses along with my younger brother and one of my uncles on the reserve. Then one day I surprised everyone by voluntarily going to a twenty-eight-day treatment centre in Fort Qu'Appelle, Saskatchewan. I told myself that maybe this would finally show everyone I was serious about changing my life. Up until now everyone kept saying things like, "This won't last. He usually gives up and goes back drinking with his friends before too long."

Everything was going great, and for the first time in my life I had my own home. It was not the newest or nicest home on the reserve, but it was mine. I was beginning to have a little pride in myself for the first time. Then one day Marilyn's mother decided she was not ready for this kind of life. She began telling me she wanted to get out and party with her old friends once in a while. She did not want to be a stay-at-home mom.

Finally, she told me she was going to Regina to see some kind of specialist, and I would have to stay home with our two small children. She caught a ride into town with one of our neighbours, and that was the last time anyone saw her for three months. She had decided her former life of partying and hanging out with her friends was more important than her own children.

Not long after this, I took our children to my mother and headed back to the city as well. Within months I was back in front of a judge, charged with assault following a barroom fight. This foolish act resulted in me spending the next six months back inside the old and much too familiar Regina Correctional Centre, the one place I said would never see me again.

In the spring of 1984 I was released, and I decided to follow my mother to the city, where she had moved along with my daughter while I was in jail. My son Anthony, who was eighteen months old at the time, stayed on the reserve with his other grandmother.

Once I arrived in the big city, it was not long before I was right back into the heavy drugs and alcohol that had been in control of my life for so many years. The downward spiral happened so fast that I did not know what I was doing half the time. I did not even know who I was partying with most of the time either; I just went along with the flow. This meant following the crowd at closing time and ending up wherever the party was.

Everything came to a crashing halt after two months of heavy partying with people I had met in the downtown area known as "skid-row." We had all been drinking heavily and popping various kinds of pills that someone had acquired from who knows where. I kept on blacking out and coming to again and again. It was not like my previous partying—this was much worse than anything I had experienced in the past.

My life was a complete mess, and I was in extremely poor health. It was not long before I found myself right back in the prison system. Considering that I spent most of my life in residential school, prison was something that unfortunately came almost naturally to me. It was almost like I had been training my entire life for this. This was the classic example of someone who was institutionalized without even realizing it.

While I was standing there in front of the judge waiting to be sent right back to the prison system that I told myself I never wanted to see again, I began to realize how pitiful I had allowed myself to become. I could barely hear a word of what he was saying. My legs were so weak that I had to force myself to stand without falling over. There was a loud buzzing in my head, and it was as though he was speaking into a cave. He sounded as though he was standing a long way off, rather than right in front of me. The last time that felt anything close to this was when I was standing in front of the priest in residential school as I was being given the strap.

For the next few years, I was angry with the entire world, and even cursed the Creator for allowing something like this to happen. I found myself involved in just about every kind of illegal activity that was available within the institution they sent me to. Once again, I became defiant toward the people in charge, and I no longer cared what they did to me. I told myself I was never going to make it through this sentence, so nothing mattered anymore.

At one point in my sentence, I even had a guard standing across from me with an AR-15 assault rifle, screaming at me to get my ass down the range that I lived on. I screamed back at him that he could go fuck himself. I was so messed up that I didn't care if he chose to shoot me or not. If all the drugs and alcohol I had been consuming couldn't kill me, then I was more than willing to let him do it. I had convinced myself that the world would be better off.

I spent most of my free time in the gym working out or beating on the heavy bag until I could barely stand up anymore. Other inmates began to see me as this crazy guy who did not give a damn about anything. Because of this attitude, most people began to avoid me rather than argue or fight with me. One guy even went as far as to tell me that he had known me for nearly five years and could not recall ever seeing me smile or laugh.

There were a few inmates that I allowed myself to become close to. They became my new family and we looked out for one another, just like the street kids that I knew a long time before. It was not long before I began meeting people that I knew from other institutions or from the streets. People whose lives were just as messed up as mine.

It wasn't until the fall of 1989 that my life took a much-needed turn back toward the Red Road. At this time, I was charged with threatening to stab and kill two correctional officers. There I was, standing in front of the warden and his team of correctional managers who were left with the job of deciding what to do with me. It did not look good for me, and they all said as much. I honestly thought that I was on my way to the Maximum-Security Unit.

They were all leaning toward sending me to the Special Handling Unit. It was at this point that an Elder I did not know took it upon himself to come to my defence. He spoke about how the Indian residential school system had caused so much confusion in young men like me, and how he felt it was his responsibility as a spiritual advisor to try to guide us back to the Red Road using the cultural and spiritual teachings given to him by his Elders.

He somehow managed to convince the warden and his managers that they should give him six months to prove his theory. He told them that after six months they could have his job if they were not satisfied with what he had accomplished. Judging from the way they were discussing my terrible prison record; I think they saw me as a challenge that this new Elder would never be able to break. They decided to give him his opportunity to fail so they could say, *See, there is nothing to these so-called spiritual teachings.*

I honestly do not know if it was my bullheadedness or that I just wanted to prove CSC wrong, but I decided I was not going to let the Elder down. From that day forward, it was like I was a changed man. I refused to let anything get to me. All the things that would normally send me into a rage no longer bothered me. I attended all the ceremonies and Healing Circles the institution allowed us to have. I became the Elder's personal helper, at his side daily from the minute he entered the institution until he went home at the end of the day.

To my surprise, I began to notice that people treated me a lot differently after a few years. People who normally did their best to avoid me like the plague were now smiling at me and saying things like "good morning" or "good afternoon" as we passed in the hallway or out in the exercise yard. People who normally gave me a wide berth were now coming up to me and shaking my hand along with that of the Elder when they left ceremonies. I noticed that I wasn't being watched as closely by security anymore. I came and went without no hassle from anyone.

There were even a few long-time staff members and guards who began telling me how they could not believe the changes they had seen in me since I began working with the Elders. They told me not to think for a minute that upper management hadn't heard about all of this either. One guard told me that my name still came up during morning briefing from time to time, but now it wasn't because of anything stupid I had done, it was because someone was praising the wonderful work I had been doing to bring about positive changes in my life.

Before long I found myself working closely with one of the two officers, I was charged with threatening a few years earlier. He was one of the people whose positive reports became essential in my transfer to a minimum-security institution a few years later. Not that this was anything I ever gave any real thought to. I was so caught up in what was happening around me that it came as a surprise when I was suddenly confronted with the idea of moving on. I guess I had become comfortable where I was.

After spending a total of eighteen years in a maximum-security institution, I was asked if I would consider transferring to a minimum-security Aboriginal Healing Lodge on the West Coast. At first, I was hesitant, but one of the Elders told me I was just afraid to move away from the place and the things that had made me feel comfortable for so long. He told me it was my old residential school thinking coming back to haunt me, and I was just going to have to learn to walk away again.

He explained that most people who have been inside for a long time become complacent and find themselves living the same daily routine over and over again. It is like they are stuck in a deep rut and cannot get out, no matter how hard they try. The sad part, he said, is that some people don't want to get out of the rut or make any attempt at creating change in their lives. These people have found a place where everything is finally going well, and they are afraid that if they change anything they will ruin everything good happening in their lives, so they choose to let the rest of the world pass them by.

In the end, my Clan Mother sat me down and explained that it would be selfish of me not to move on and share the teachings I had been given over the previous few years. She told me that maybe there was someone over there who really needed to hear what I had to say to move on with their life. She explained that if in my lifetime I successfully help only one person to move forward in a positive and healthy way with the teachings I received, I will have done enough to make both her and the Creator happy. When she put it like that, there was no way I could say no.

After years of learning from my Elders and spiritual advisors, I had finally accepted that I needed to turn my life over to the Creator if I was going to stop living in the "poor me" state I was stuck in for so many years. Sooner or later we all have to stop feeling sorry for ourselves and start rebuilding the damage we have caused around us. This is the only way we will ever find the happiness we seek in life. No one is going to come along and hand it to us; we have to work for it like everything else. She told me that I would get out what I choose to put into it.

Like so many of my fellow survivors who were also fortunate enough to find the strength to turn and walk away from that old lifestyle, where we were at the mercy of our substance abuse issues, I too was unable to see the reality of the troubled world I found myself trapped in. Perhaps I was too willing to accept the colonial beliefs that were constantly being pushed onto us by the churches and the federal government, beliefs like how First Nations people are not as valuable in society as the dominant white population, and that we will never amount to anything of value.

Only since finding my way back to the sacred teachings of our ancestors have, I begun to clearly see the damage that has been inflicted upon the First Nations people of this country. It has only been within the last ten years that I have begun to understand why people refer to the residential schools as another form of genocide against us.

It is as though a curtain has been drawn back and I have begun to see, through clear eyes, our people living in poverty. I can finally see the many social issues that plague our nations: the unemployment rates, the child-welfare cases, the rising suicide rates, the addictions, the low levels of education, and the poor housing conditions that our people live in, both on and off their reserves. I have seen how we are rapidly losing our languages and cultural teachings within our communities.

These systemic issues have caused negative impacts on our people for generations, and can easily be traced to colonization, the residential schools and the Sixties Scoop. These issues can also be linked to the high number of Aboriginal people within the Canadian correctional system, which has sadly become known to the First Nations people as the modern-day replacement for the residential school system. When I began learning about the Seven Sacred Teachings from my Elders, I was told to keep in mind that it is also our duty to ensure that the road we walk is always smoother for those who follow us, meaning we should not allow ourselves to be filled with anger and frustration over the many terrible things we have experienced throughout our lifetime. Instead, we must follow the sacred teachings and learn to forgive those who have wronged us in any way. We must learn to teach others, so they do not make the same mistakes we have made along the way.

Because of these wonderful teachings I have been given by the loving and caring teachers and their families over the past thirty years, I no longer allow myself to feel anger and hatred toward the people who have negatively impacted my life. Instead, I choose to do as my Elders have taught me and simply take a few minutes to pray for these people, asking the Creator to be kind to them and help them see the things they have done. This is all part of learning how to be humble and kind to ourselves, as well as to others.

My Elders have always told me to remember one important thing: always practice what you preach. They have taught me that it does not matter what your life was like when you were on the Dark Path, because the Creator sees the sincerity in what you are doing now, and he knows you are trying to better yourself. That is all he expects from any of us. We have to lead by example so the next seven generations to come will know what is expected from them as well. This is all part of the continuing circle of life.

We all have to stop hating ourselves and accept the fact that all the awful things we have experienced throughout our short lives were meant to teach us how to be better human beings. If we choose to go on hating ourselves and the sometimes-terrible pasts we came from, we will never heal and move forward. Instead, we will find ourselves stuck in a world we want so desperately to get away from.

I recall driving through the East Side of Vancouver one summer evening on my way to the Friendship Centre. I was with an Elder from the Healing Lodge on the Chehalis Indian reserve. He was taking me to a weekly event known as "West Coast Night." This consisted of a gathering involving all the West Coast people who resided within the city of Vancouver and the surrounding area. It was their night to gather as a community so they could practice and showcase their traditional singing and dancing.

As we made our way to the Friendship Centre, the Elder wanted me to see the infamous East Side of Vancouver, where all the poorest people reside. This area has the worst reputation in the country for crime and drug abuse. Every day there are literally dozens of deaths due to drug overdoses and other assorted drug- and alcohol-related crimes. Everything had changed so much since I last visited the area that I could barely recognize anything down there. This was not the Vancouver from my memories.

As we slowly drove through the area, the Elder told me to take a good look at the people, because all of them were lost. As he pointed out the large number of First Nations people, he said, "They have all lost their spirits, and that is why they cannot get away from this place. Unless someone with strong spiritual teachings comes along and guides them back to the Red Road, they will probably remain lost forever. I know these words are the truth, because I too was once lost, and it took a strong Elder to bring me back to the right path."

When the Elder was done talking, I found my mind wandering back to my first visit to a big house. This was with the Leon family on the Chehalis reserve. I can remember the sounds around me when the drummers began singing and drumming heavily at the same time. There had to be at least fifteen to twenty of them drumming in unison. It was as though the sound was vibrating through my entire body, and I could feel all the hair on the back of my neck standing up. There were screams that came when one of the young female dancers, who was seated a few feet in front of me, began to call out to her spirit. Her cries were like those of someone screaming out in pain and agony. This almost brought me to my knees, and I could feel my heart racing. Even though this was not my own culture, I knew the significance of what she was doing. She was calling to her spirit and asking for its strength and guidance, just as I had done on numerous occasions while sitting alone in my small lodge participating in my Vision Quest ceremonies.

Despite all the turmoil I have experienced throughout my lifetime, I have learned to accept the path the Creator has chosen for me. Every morning when I rise and prepare for the new day,

I begin by thanking him for granting me another beautiful day, regardless of what it is like outside. The most important thing is that I am truly grateful for his gifts, and I will try my hardest to remain humble for the rest of the day.

When I say my morning prayers, I always give thanks for the medicines and food that Mother Earth provides to keep us alive. Then I say a prayer for all the sick people who are stuck in their hospital beds, and those who are institutionalized and cannot get out to do this for themselves. Before ending my prayer, I take time to recognize our Elders and their families. Then I ask the Creator to forgive me if I have made any mistakes and ask him to take away anything bad or negative that may be headed toward us.

I do these things even though there is no one around to witness what I am doing, or to hear the words I am putting out there. I do not do any of this for recognition or thanks, I do it because it is what the Creator expects of me. It is how my ancestors have done it for thousands of years, and the most important part is that it makes me feel good inside.

When I think back to my childhood and begin talking about things that were taken away from me, I realize how important it is to pass these teachings on to our future generations. Even though it is true that we live under the influence of the more dominant European society, we have to maintain pride in who we are as a people and where we come from. If we fail to do so, we will lose our identity and end up wandering aimlessly, like all those poor people I had witnessed wandering on the East Side.

We must continuously do our best to remain vigilant and not lose our focus, because there are still a lot of people out there who are trying to undermine us and what we believe in—people such as Senator Lynn Beyak, formerly of the Conservative Party, who went on national television and made the ridiculous statement that Aboriginal people need to focus on the good things that residential schools did for their people. There was nothing good about residential schools. There is never anything good about genocide or the abuse of children.

This same senator later made the statement that if the First Nations people want things to improve for them, they need to trade in their status cards for Canadian citizenship. Maybe this individual needs to take a closer look at where her own ancestors came from and consider returning there. Anyone who doesn't understand how lucky they are to be here in Indian Country should consider packing up and returning to their own ancestral lands.

People like this need to wake up and realize that the First Nations people were here long before this was even a country. In fact, maybe everyone who wants to stay should be asking for a status card. I can't help thinking about something an Elder once told me. He said we will never be able to fully understand where we are headed until we understand where we have been. Too bad that this racist senator can't understand something as simple as this.

A lot of the First Nations people who heard this senator speak took to the various media outlets to vent their frustrations, and to ask for this senator's immediate resignation. That evening numerous survivors appeared on the APTN national news to say that there were no good things that happened in those schools, other than the closings.

They went on to say that when you attempt to conduct a genocide in the name of God, it does not excuse the wrongs that were committed. Another person asked if this was the Conservative Party's honest idea of Truth and Reconciliation. I guess all we can do is pray for this lady, just like our Elders have always taught us to do. I for one will not stoop to her level. My Elders have taught me better.

When you look at the news stories that are continuously being flashed all over the television, you begin to understand what a messed-up world we live in. These terrible events aren't just limited to North America, they are happening all over the world. Innocent people are dying by the hundreds of thousands every day, all in the name of one religion or another.

When I was released from prison in 2008 and allowed to slowly reintegrate into society, I saw things much differently than I did when I went inside. This time I knew the importance of our Elders and the cultural and spiritual teachings they had to offer. I was afraid to even think about what would happen to me if I was once again forced to live without all of the teachings, I was fortunate enough to have been provided with.

Two years earlier, in 2006, I was permitted to attend a four-day Sundance ceremony in Merritt, BC. It was while there that I made a commitment to live my life in accordance with the Seven Sacred Teachings of our people. While holding the Sacred Pipe and standing before the Sacred Tree, I promised I would never again touch drugs or alcohol. I gave flesh offerings and prayed for every person I had ever victimized during my lifetime.

When my time to reintegrate arrived, I was invited to one of the big houses and given words of encouragement by my Elders there. They told me I was once again like a baby who was about to step out into the world for the first time. I was told to expect to stumble from time to time, but that I always had the teachings and support I needed to get back up again. These are words I will always carry with me, and I know there is always support there if I need it. I just have to know when to ask.

The anger and hatred I once carried for the Church, and anyone connected to that form of religion has all but disappeared. I will never completely forget about the abuse I suffered in their residential schools, but I do not allow this to control my thoughts and emotions anymore. I have learned the importance of moving on in a healthy and respectful way. This is what my Elders taught me over the years, and I am truly grateful for their gift. I will live by these teachings until the day I die.

It took me a long time to wake up and realize there are a lot of wonderful teachings available to us, we just have to open our hearts and minds. Despite the negativity I have lived through, I am confident that, with the help of our Elders and their teachings, we can finally begin to repair the sacred family circles that have been all but destroyed by taking away the children and forcing them into the residential school system.

When we begin our healing, we must keep in mind that it took many generations to get to where we are today. Therefore, we must keep in mind that the road to healing will also take generations. I may no longer carry the anger and hatred I held on to for most of my life, but I will always remember that these negative emotions were the main reason for my life of substance abuse.

Whenever I think back to my years spent in residential school, the one memory that sticks out the most is the sheer loneliness that was experienced by so many. Not just me, but so many of the young who were forcefully taken from their loving families far too early in life. I can easily recall those sad little faces sitting on the wooden benches surrounding the playroom as we waited for the supervisor to holler his instructions.

When I looked at the smallest children, there was often fear in their eyes. These were the ones who often bore the brunt of everything. Because they were so small, they would often miss out when fruit or snacks were being handed out. They would get pushed to the end of the line when lunch or dinner was called. I knew exactly how they felt, because I too went through the same thing when I arrived at age five. I was forced to grow up fast or continue being bullied.

As I got older, I did my best to look out for the smallest boys. This would cause problems, because I would usually end up having to fight with some of the older ones. Luckily this only went on for a short period, because they quickly realized I would stand up to them regardless of the outcome, and it usually meant minor injuries to both sides. Eventually they figured out that it wasn't worth the effort to continuously get into confrontations with me, so many of the older boys began helping me ensure that the little guys weren't being pushed out of the way anymore.

Although the last of these notorious schools in Canada finally closed its doors for good in the early 1980s, the awful memories that went along with so many of them still remain as strong as ever. Thanks in part to the tens of thousands of survivors who are still alive today, these tragic stories will remain alive for future generations to hear and continue to pass on to their children. Any survivor you ask will tell you they want to keep these terrible memories alive to prevent this kind of atrocity from occurring again.

Some of those old school buildings remain standing in a broken-down, derelict state, while others have been torn down to help with the healing of the community. Even with the old buildings gone, you will often see people standing there in silence, offering prayers and making small tobacco offerings. This is their way of not only honouring the brothers and sisters who suffered there, but of keeping the children's memories alive.

This is something that I often do when I visit one of the many old school sites that are still standing. Whenever I walk through some of these dilapidated and rundown buildings that have been long abandoned by society, I can't help but cringe. Standing in the long-abandoned hallways, I only have to close my eyes to recall the sounds of the children who once roamed the now empty halls.

Luckily, in my home community the residents of the reserve did not want to see Marieval going to waste. The Department of Indian and Northern Affairs went into partnership with the local First Nations Bands and took over the facility. The first thing they did was renovate the existing structures before adding a new gymnasium and larger classroom areas. This put our once-hated school on par with the modern public schools in the surrounding communities.

Today it has become our community school with our own staff and teachers, most of whom are of First Nation descent. This turned the old Church-run school into something positive that now gives back to the community. People from the area now look upon the old site with pride, because they took something seen as negative and turned it into something they can be proud of. Even most of the school curriculum takes into consideration that the students are of First Nation descent. Today you will even find that the ones who help to run the school and care for it are former students.

Despite the fact that there were some good memories that went along with our stay in those schools, it is always easier to recall the traumatic memories. This same rule will apply when dealing with groups of young children from any corner of the world. When they are traumatized for lengthy periods, these events will eventually dominate their thoughts and dreams, eventually pushing the few good memories farther into the back of their minds, making them harder to access.

This is something I can personally say is true, because I suffered through eleven painful years in two of those terrible schools. Whenever someone questions any of my memories regarding my stay in residential school, I tell them I lived these horrible memories long enough to know what is reality and what is fiction. When I was finally old enough to get myself out of that school system, I went on to experience vivid nightmares for many years, so no one can convince me that my memories are wrong.

I often wonder if the people who sit in their ivory towers in Ottawa ever seriously think about the depth of damage that has been done to our First Nations people. I have on more than one occasion seen people, most of whom I would consider to be Elders, standing on the old school site in silence with tears streaming down their faces as they recall old friends who are now long gone, or personal incidents they cannot forget.

Like I've said before, I used to get angry whenever I would hear any of the non-Native people saying it was time for the First Nations people to get over it and move on with life. Finally, an Elder told me to relax and think about it, because the person was right in a way. The Elder told me that the next time I hear someone make a derogatory statement like this, I should tell him, "You know what, you're right, and that's why we're working on it."

When I was living in Kamloops, I often went for walks along the mountain overlooking the old residential school. Sometimes I would sit there along the hillside and contemplate whether I even wanted to begin writing any of these painful memories. Part of me said that I had to speak up, that it was in fact my duty to say something. Then there was that other part that wanted to do its best to forget about everything that happened and quietly move on.

This is the side that was afraid people would laugh at me and tell me to shut up and get back to the reserve where I belong. They might even tell me I was an embarrassment to my people, just like I heard them do to some of the old drunk men sitting on the street bench in the city.

For the longest time I went back and forth, unable to resolve the issue, then one day someone asked if I would help them write something for the Truth and Reconciliation Commission that was touring the province. When I finished helping him write his submission, I began writing my own. Before I realized it, I had written close to a hundred pages, and people began telling me it was really good and that I should consider having it published.

After some long talks with my Elders, some of whom were survivors themselves, I sat down and did some editing and rewriting, mainly because I did not want to focus primarily on the horror stories that caused so much of the anger toward the churches. Instead, I chose to place most of my energy on talking about the things I did to heal and move forward in a good way.

My only hope was that if I did it this way, I would give other survivors the opportunity to see that returning to our culture and spirituality is something worth trying. After all, no one is going to tell any of us that we cannot talk about these things anymore, because those days are long gone. Today, all our cultural and spiritual beliefs and practices are protected under the Canadian Charter of Rights and Freedoms. As a result, most of our sacred ceremonies are growing stronger every year.

I often remind myself that I could have easily chosen to spend the remainder of my days in the drunken stupor I once had for a life, focusing all my energy on being angry at the world for what had been done to me as a child. Instead, I chose to tell anyone who will listen what I did to help myself.

Today, whenever I am sitting in a group or talking with other survivors, I remind myself how easy it would be to allow myself to stumble and end up right back on that negative path. I am thankful for all the harsh lessons I have received from living that negative lifestyle, and for the fact that I know I can easily end up back there. This knowledge is what keeps me clean and sober today. It has given me the much-needed strength and desire to heal.

Sometimes when I am talking with my friends, they tell me that if they were in my shoes, and they had to go through everything I have gone through, they don't think they would be able to forgive and move on. This is when I explain to them that they have to practice the teachings that much harder, because like the Elders always tell us, "Everything that happens to us in life happens for a reason." Usually, it is to teach us something about ourselves.

Most people find it difficult to comprehend this kind of thinking, but it has worked this way for hundreds of years, if not longer. Without teachings like this, maybe our ancestors would not have had the strength to overcome the many attempts at cultural genocide that were made against our people. Without the sacred teachings, perhaps I would not have the strength or ability to begin repairing the broken circle that makes up my life.

We are always being told that we do not have the right to judge others, so we have to learn to be patient and humble. If we learn how to do this one simple thing, we will find that things don't make us as angry anymore, which in turn is good for us, because people who are angry all the time end up with high blood pressure and all sorts of other health issues. That alone should tell you that negativity is no good for anyone. So just let things go and move on.

Today I have an Elder who everyone tells me is the most patient man they have ever known. Maybe he can teach me something about humility. Someone even told me that they have known him all their life, and they can't remember hearing him get angry or upset about anything. They say that he just smiles and says something like, "Oh well, maybe tomorrow will be better." With that in mind I will say, "All my relations!" and I hope that you all have a better day tomorrow.

All my relations,

Ta'wacine O'hitika